DANGEROUS SNAKES

DANGEROUS SNAKES
OF AUSTRALIA

REVISED EDITION

Peter Mirtschin / Richard Davis

NH
NEW HOLLAND

Cover photograph:
Taipan *Oxyuranus scutellatus scutellatus*

First published in the UK in 1992 by
New Holland (Publishers) Ltd
37 Connaught Street, London W2 2AZ

ISBN 1 85368 209 8

Printed in Singapore by Kyodo Printing Co (S'pore) Pte Ltd

Cover photograph: Taipan *Oxyuranus scutellatus scutellatus*

CONTENTS

ACKNOWLEDGMENTS

South Australian Government for financial assistance in the form of a Conservation Grant which subsidised travel costs necessary for photographs.

The authors are indebted to Greg Johnston for his patience and skill in converting head photographs by P. Mirtschin to line drawings. Greg also assisted with the distribution maps.

For providing valuable snake specimens for photographs, the authors would like to thank: Brian Barnett; Arthur Watts; Barry Searle; Eric Worrell of the Australian Reptile Park; Graeme Gow; Joe Bredl of Bredl's Reptile Park; Harry Ehman; G. Coombe of the South Australian National Parks and Wildlife Service; Roy Pails; Mike Van der Straaten; Neil Charles; Peter Richardson of the Dreamtime Reptile Park; Darryl Levi.

Peter Rawlinson for line drawings of scale counting techniques and head scalation of the Red-bellied Black Snake.

Steve Wilson for providing photographs of Tanners Brown Snake and Butlers Snake and M. Gillam for the photograph of the Speckled Brown Snake.

Mike Tyler for constructive review of the conservation section.

Gwynne Hughes for assistance in obtaining specimens of the Inland Taipan.

Stan for cartoons.

South Australian Bureau of Meteorology for isohyet, isothermal, and rainfall information.

Struan Sutherland for his assistance with information regarding venoms and snake-bite treatment.

Alan Broad for information on venoms.

Jeanette Covacevich for assistance with information on Queensland snakes and the Inland Taipan.

Adrienne Edwards who helped in photographing heads

of some of the preserved specimens for head drawings.

John Lydeamore for assistance with map preparation.

Harold Cogger for his review of Chapters 1, 2, 4, and 5.

Dave Polglase for a grammatical review of the manuscript.

Marion Billings, Patty Davis, and Lyn Altman, each of whom typed some of the manuscript.

G. M. Storr who provided distribution data on the Western Australian snakes covered in this book.

Tasmanian Museum and Art Gallery for distribution data.

Queen Victoria Museum and Art Gallery, Tasmania, for distribution data.

For conservation status we are thankful to: National Parks and Wildlife Service, New South Wales; Department of Fisheries and Wildlife, Western Australia; Conservation Commission, Northern Territory; National Parks and Wildlife Service, Tasmania; Fisheries and Wildlife, Victoria; National Parks and Wildlife Service, Queensland; National Parks and Wildlife Service, South Australia.

Commonwealth Serum Laboratories for information and photographs concerning antivenom production.

T. Schwaner for manuscript review.

Special thanks to the officers of the South Australian National Parks and Wildlife Service who assisted in obtaining specimens from interstate, for photographs.

The *Medical Journal of Australia* for permission to publish 'Skull features of Elapids', N. Hamilton Fairley, 1929.

Doug Henderson, Pathologist, Flinders Medical Centre, for photographing the snake's fang.

M. Hutchinson for supplying head photographs of the Highland Copperhead for head drawings.

Herpetologists P. Hudson, H. Nygren, P. Fennell, Hans Van Dyk, W. Ingall, for assistance on field trips and other support.

J. Bredl junior for his patience in teaching Peter Mirtschin the skills of snake handling.

G. Harold for the photograph of the Northern Death Adder and assistance in obtaining the head drawings.

INTRODUCTION

The dangerous venomous snakes are a fascinating part of Australia's unique wildlife. Undoubtedly, they are the most poisonous snakes in the world. Why are they so venomous and what is their place in the ecology of our continent? The present authors do not believe that 'the only good snake is a dead one', but that venomous snakes, like all animals, play an important role in our environment.

The fact remains, however, that these creatures are dangerous, and their bite may result in death. It is right and proper, therefore, that they be treated with respect and not handled by amateurs. Through greater understanding of our venomous animals and through recent research into the management of snake bite, particularly by Dr Struan Sutherland and his team at the Commonwealth Serum Laboratories in Melbourne, the outlook for snake-bite victims in Australia has significantly improved. It appears that this same research has led to the improved management of other animal bites, such as spider bite and bee sting, both in Australia and overseas.

Snake venoms are extremely complex mixtures of proteins and enzymes, all with different actions. It is likely that in the future some of these components will be isolated and found to be important. The anticoagulant fractions may be useful for our Red Cross blood banks. The neuromuscular blocking components may be useful for anaesthesia or treating tetanus. So vast and varied are the proteins that even a cure for some cancers may be hidden in the venoms, waiting for an enthusiastic researcher to isolate it. In medicine the study of venoms has repeatedly led to greater understanding of human physiology and pharmacology.

We believe that it is time the general public questioned

9

the tradition of killing every snake possible. Emotional, front-page reporting of snake bites by our newspapers is unfortunately a colourful, rather extreme view of the true situation. Actually, snake bite is a rare phenomenon and the prognosis for its victims has been greatly improved.

We hope this book will

- Provide information and a key for identifying dangerous snakes.

- Stimulate recognition of the need for the conservation of our venomous snakes.

- Act as a reference book for first aid and hospital management of snake-bite victims.

PETER J. MIRTSCHIN
RICHARD DAVIS

PART ONE

SNAKES: IDENTIFICATION AND CONSERVATION

Chapter 1
THE RELATIVE DANGER OF AUSTRALIAN TERRESTRIAL SNAKES

There are thirty different species of dangerously venomous snakes in Australia and for various reasons it is difficult to list them in order of their relative danger to human beings. The net effect of a snake bite depends on the combination of many factors. These can be divided into victim factors, snake factors, and management factors.

Victim factors	Snake factors	Management factors
age	size	first aid
weight	venom toxicity	hospital management
health	number of bites	
body chemistry	whether venom inoculated	
	volume of venom inoculated	

Table 1.1   *Factors affecting snake bite*

Snake bite is more serious in the very old and the very young. In particular, bites occurring in small children are not uncommon and are very serious. Victims who enjoy good health are less likely to be seriously affected than others. Some people are allergic to snake venom and a major allergic reaction, called anaphylaxis, may occur immediately following a bite. This idiosyncrasy is more likely to occur in allergic individuals and also people who have been bitten previously, such as herpetologists.

A bite from a large adult snake is potentially more dangerous than one from a small juvenile snake. There is variation, too, in the toxicity of snake venoms:[1, 2] very

13

poisonous snakes include the Taipans, Death Adders, Tiger Snakes, Brown Snakes and Copperheads, while the Black Snakes are less venomous.

Other snake factors include their biting mechanisms and their venom yields. The number and effectiveness of the bites are also important.

Victims who receive correct first aid measures, who are transported to hospital quickly, and whose medical management is satisfactory, naturally will suffer less. Correct treatment does decrease snake-bite morbidity and mortality.

The Queensland Museum has produced danger scores for 'Australia's Most Dangerous Snakes' by rating five aspects of snake bite.[3] They are:

1. venom toxicity
2. venom yield
3. fang length
4. temperament
5. frequency of bite

Each component carries a maximum of 5 points and varies from snake to snake.

A rating score for Australia's venomous snakes can be derived using this scoring system. The following list illustrates this method.

Taipan	21
Mulga or King Brown Snake	16
Death Adder	15
Common Brown Snake	14
Tiger Snake	14
Inland Taipan	12
Colletts Snake	10
Western Brown Snake	10
Copperhead	10
Bass Strait Island Tiger Snakes	9
Red-bellied Black Snake	9
Spotted Black Snake	8
Rough-scaled Snake	7
Dugite	6
Small-eyed Snake	6

While the scale is useful in predicting the probability of a serious bite from these snakes, for the victim this scale is meaningless. In evaluating the seriousness of a particular bite, it is irrelevant that in Australia the frequency of bites due to one species of snake is higher than another. The snake factors that will affect the seriousness of the victim's bite are the amount and toxicity of the venom inoculated.

The Commonwealth Serum Laboratories have conducted considerable research into the comparable toxicity of Australia's poisonous snakes. Standardised conditions for venom collection are used. Following collection by milking, the venom is immediately freeze-dried and stored in a vacuum. This prevents loss of venom potency due to bacterial attack, which will occur if the venom is kept in a liquid form while awaiting drying. Mice are used for the tests and the venom is prepared in saline solution. The lethal dose (LD_{50}) for mice is calculated and this is used to compare the toxicity of the various snake species. The lethal dose (LD_{50}) is defined as that dose of venom which will result in the death of 50 per cent of test subjects. The values have been determined by the Commonwealth Serum Laboratories and are expressed in mg/kg for laboratory mice.

The relative danger of the venomous Australian snakes can be compared by reviewing the 'rating' given to each snake. This rating takes into account both the toxicity of the venom and the average venom yield. Blank spaces indicate where additional work has to be carried out. A low toxicity figure (LD_{50}) indicates a very poisonous snake.

Clearly it is necessary to take into consideration venom yield as well as venom toxicity. If one considered only the LD_{50} it would appear that the average consequences of a bite from a Common Brown Snake would be worse than from a Taipan. It is well known that this is not the case, and it is because the venom yield of the Taipan, on average, is sixty times that of the Common Brown Snake. Hence the significance of a Taipan bite (when tested on mice) is about forty times more serious than that of the Common Brown Snake.

Common Name	Scientific name	Toxicity LD$_{50}$ mg/kg (mice)[2]	Av. yield mg	Rating (mice) (total LD$_{50}$ doses)
Inland Taipan	*Oxyuranus microlepidotus*	0·010	44·2[4]	218000
Taipan	*Oxyuranus scutellatus scutellatus*	0·064	120[5]	95000
Reevesby Island Tiger Snake	*Notechis ater niger*	0·099	34·3[6]	18000
Common Tiger Snake	*Notechis scutatus*	0·118	35[7]	15000
Western Tiger Snake	*Notechis ater occidentalis*	0·124	35[8]	14500
Chappell Island Tiger Snake	*Notechis ater serventyi*	0·271	75[7]	14000
Tasmanian and King Island Tiger Snake	*Notechis ater humphreysi*			
Kreffts Tiger Snake	*Notechis ater ater*		23[9]	
Common Brown Snake	*Pseudonaja textilis textilis*	0·040	2[5]	2500
Western Brown Snake	*Pseudonaja nuchalis*	0·338		
Peninsula Brown Snake	*Pseudonaja textilis inframacula*			
Dugite	*Pseudonaja affinis affinis*	0·560		
Tanners Brown Snake	*Pseudonaja affinis tanneri*			
Speckled Brown Snake	*Pseudonaja guttata*		0·5[10]	
Ingrams Brown Snake	*Pseudonaja ingrami*			

Mulga Snake	Pseudechis australis	1·91	180[11]	5000
Red-bellied Black Snake	Pseudechis porphyriacus	2·53	35[12]	700
Spotted Black Snake	Pseudechis guttatus	1·53	30[12]	1000
Colletts Snake	Pseudechis colletti	2·38 (saline)	30[10]	600 approx
Butlers Snake	Pseudechis butleri			
Common Death Adder	Acanthophis antarcticus	0·338	78[2]	12000
Desert Death Adder	Acanthophis pyrrhus			
Northern Death Adder	Acanthophis praelongus			
Stephens Banded Snake	Hoplocephalus stephensi	1·44		
Broad-headed Snake	Hoplocephalus bungaroides			
Pale-headed Snake	Hoplocephalus bitorquatus		1·66[9]	
Copperhead (lowland)	Austrelaps superbus	0·500	24·9[13]	2500
Copperhead (highland)				
Copperhead (pygmy)				
Rough-scaled Snake	Tropidechis carinatus	1·09	6[11]	300
Small-eyed Snake	Cryptophis nigrescens	2·67 (saline)	8[14]	150 approx

Table 1.2   *The relative danger of Australian terrestrial snakes*

The yield of venom collected during milking snakes varies greatly. For instance, a Black Tiger Snake from Kangaroo Island, which is kept at Whyalla, consistently yields about 60 mg of venom. This snake is unusually aggressive and bites into the rubber-topped vial with great enthusiasm. This yield is about 1·6 times the average yield for Tiger Snakes.

It must be remembered that the figures shown in Table 1.2 are all based on the effects of the venoms on mice. When tested on other laboratory animals the results vary. For example, work carried out by the Commonwealth Serum Laboratories in 1937, determined that the venom of the Reevesby Island Tiger Snake was 2·3 times more deadly than the Common Tiger Snake venom when tested on guinea-pigs.[6] The latest results on mice suggest it is only 1·2 times more deadly.[2] It is clear, therefore, that the effect of the venom on different animals varies considerably. (See Table 1.3)

It is impossible to determine the toxicity figures and ratings of venomous snakes for humans, and it would be wrong to extrapolate directly data from animal experiments and draw conclusions for humans. Varying toxicity figures for different laboratory animals are illustrated in Table 1.3.

	Guinea pig	Rabbit	Mouse	Sheep	Rat
Tiger Snake	0·02	0·05	0·25	0·01	0·4
Black Snake	2·5	0·6		0·8	2·5
Spotted Black Snake	0·6	0·6–1	2·5		0·7
Death Adder	0·15	0·15	0·7	0·025	
Copperhead	0·06	0·7	1·2	0·1	1·4
Common Brown Snake		0·2			

Table 1.3 *Lethal doses of snake venoms for various laboratory animals (mg/kg)*[15]

Chapter 2
THE MORPHOLOGY OF THE DANGEROUS SNAKES

Order   SQUAMATA
Sub-order   SERPENTES
Family   Elapidae

Two separate sub-orders of the order SQUAMATA exist. They are the lizards, sub-order SAURIA, (see photographs, pages 33 and 34) and snakes, sub-order SERPENTES. The distinction between the two sub-orders relies on the possession of a number of features and is summarised in Table 2.1.

Feature	SAURIA (lizards)	SERPENTES (snakes)
Limbs	present	absent
Eyelids	present	absent
External ear	present	absent
Enlarged ventral scales	absent	present
Anterior brain case	open	closed
Jaw connection	rigid	flexible
Tongue	short and fleshy	long, bifurcated
Lungs	two	one
Regeneration of tail	present	absent

Table 2.1   *Differences between snakes and lizards*

Although there are exceptions to these rules, all lizards and all snakes possess most of the features in their respective category. The absence of limbs in snakes allows them to slide along in search of prey creating minimal disturbance. The possession of legs would hinder their movement through grass, cracks, burrows, and leaf litter. The snake's brain is completely enclosed in the bone of the skull, affording it optimum protection during struggles, biting, and clawing of the prey. With a flexible jaw connection that distends the ligament connecting the upper and lower jaw, snakes are able to swallow prey much larger than their head size, offsetting the disadvantage of not being able to chew their food into small pieces.

Snakes in Australia fall into six families:

Typhlopidae	Blind snakes
Boidae	Pythons
Acrochordidae	File snakes
Colubridae	Harmless snakes with no fangs, or rear-fanged snakes
Hydrophiidae	Sea snakes
Elapidae	Front-fanged snakes

It is the last family, the Elapidae, that includes the dangerous Australian terrestrial snakes.

The following characteristics, while fitting many of the Australian snake types, specifically refer to the dangerous terrestrial elapid genera.

Senses

Smell

The olfactory system is a combination of nostrils, bifurcated tongue, and the Jacobsons organ. Snakes can use the nostrils separately by drawing air into the sensory chamber or can smell by collecting scent molecules with the tongue and transferring them to the paired Jacobsons organ in the roof of the mouth. The function of this organ was originally for smelling mouth contents but later evolved for testing airborne smells.[16]

The sense of smell is the most acute sense in snakes.

Vision

Eyesight is an important complement to smell when hunting, and in snakes is more attuned to the movement of objects. It is possible for a snake to slide past a motionless prey or an enemy without even seeing it. Snakes can be induced to strike at an assortment of objects once they have detected the scent of familiar prey.

Focusing only appears to be possible at short range and may not even be sharp compared with human eyesight.

The eyeball is spherical in shape and in most cases the pupil is round. Death Adders, which are mainly nocturnal, have vertical pupils which allow greater expansion in the dark, thus producing vastly improved night vision.

Taste

Taste buds are known to be present in snakes, though the extent of tasting ability is more or less unknown.[17]

Hearing

Human ears detect sound by shock waves, travelling at high or low frequencies through air, which impinge on a membrane or drum inside the ear. Snakes have no such mechanism and are therefore insensitive to any airborne sound. Unlike many other native animals, snakes can be observed in the wild without restrictions on human speech, since they just can't hear this type of sound.

Snakes can detect ground vibrations resulting from larger animals walking in their vicinity.

Food and feeding

Various snakes use different methods to catch their prey. The technique also varies according to the type of prey. Brown Snakes feed mainly on reptiles and so their prey-immobilising technique has evolved to include constriction as well as venom injection. Even when catching mammalian prey, they still use the same combination. Taipans use a snap bite then hold off, waiting for the prey to die before going in to devour it. Death Adders and Tiger Snakes often hang on while their prey succumbs to the venom and then swallow it. (See photographs, page 35.)

The prey is eaten by allowing the lower jaw (mandible) to disconnect via an elastic ligament, so allowing animals larger than the snake's head to be swallowed. The curved teeth on each side of the jaw appear to creep forward alternately as the prey is forced or pulled down the neck. The palatine teeth hold the prey in position while the mandibular teeth are disconnected from the prey and then advanced along the prey. The post-maxillary teeth are then advanced alternately along the prey's length.

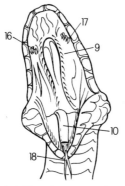

Death Adder — Jaws apart, showing the fangs, post maxillary and ptery-gopalatine teeth

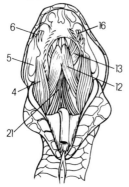

Death Adder — Dissection of the roof of the mouth, illustrating the essential muscles involved in the mechanism of bite

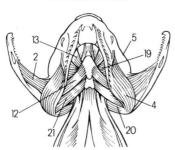

Tiger Snake — Dissection of the roof of the mouth after separation of the mandibles

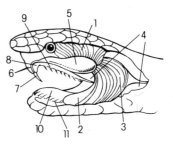

Death Adder — Superficial dissection, showing poison gland

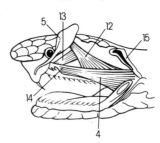

Death Adder — Deep dissection, with gland everted

1. Anterior temporal muscle
2. Anterior temporal muscle (mandibular portion)
3. Posterior temporal muscle
4. External pterygoid
5. Poison gland
6. Poison duct
7. Grooved fang (see page 39)
8. *Vagina dentis*
9. Pterygo-palatine teeth
10. Trachea
11. Recurved mandibular teeth
12. Spheno-pterygoid muscle
13. Spheno- or parieto-palatine muscle
14. External process of the ecto-pterygoid into which the external pterygoid muscle is inserted
15. The quadrate bone
16. Reserve fang
17. Post-maxillary teeth
18. Forked tongue
19. Parieto-pterygoid muscle
20. Digastric muscle
21. Sub-occipital articular muscle (Dugès)

A variety of prey types are eaten. Shine (1977), found that in the highlands of eastern Australia, Tiger Snakes, Black Snakes, Brown Snakes and Copperheads utilised lizards and frogs most frequently[18]. He attributed this to the lack of mammalian fauna in Australia. Despite such restrictions, snakes are generally opportunistic feeders and a large range of food is taken. Taipans prefer mammals and King Brown Snakes will eat other snakes. Common Brown Snakes and Copperheads are reported by Worrell as being cannibalistic.[7] Very little invertebrate food is taken and it is doubtful that elapid snakes ever feed deliberately on these animals.

Locomotion

Snakes use co-ordinated muscular action, which lifts small sections of the body only slightly, to move their ventral scales into contact with the ground. Contact resistance enables the snake to push itself forward. Each part of the snake's body passes over the same spot. This attribute allows the snake to move around objects on the ground with least disturbance, which is a big asset in hunting.

When moving through water the latter part of the snake is used as a paddle that is moved from side to side, thus propelling the snake forward in a zig-zag fashion.

Sloughing (skin shedding)

Periodically as the skin ages and wears or as the snake grows, it sheds the outer dead epidermal layer.

About a week before sloughing, a mucus-like fluid is excreted beneath the old skin, the skin's outward appearance becomes dull, and the eyes develop a white milky coloration. (See photograph, page 36.)

During this period the snake appears to be uncomfortable, and can often be heard to suffer some respiratory discomfort as slight mucus blockages occur in the nasal passages. A few days before shedding the skin, the eyes become clearer and eventually the snake begins to rub its nose on rough surfaces until the skin peels off the head, and the snake wriggles out of the old skin, using any debris to gain purchase and to provide friction for its removal. As the skin comes off it is turned inside out and is longer than the length of the snake[19]. The mucus secretion serves as a lubricant in the skin's removal. (See photographs, page 36.)

Skins are shed more frequently in young snakes as they grow. Food availability affects growth rate and therefore the frequency of sloughing.

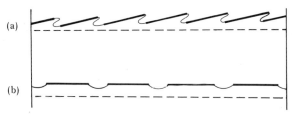

Diagram 2 *Snake skin (a) before shedding (b) after shedding*

Reproduction

Male snakes have a paired sex organ which is sheathed at the base of the tail, and for this reason, on average, the caudal section is wider and longer than for females of the same species.

The male hemipenes are turned inside out when everted and often possess a series of pointed spines. (See photograph, page 37.) Only one of the hemipenes is used during copulation.

Mating observations in the wild are rare and most information to hand is the result of captive studies. Most southern snakes are reported to mate in spring, but some have been noted to mate in autumn. From reproduction studies undertaken in 1977 by Shine[20], autumn matings of both the Mulga Snake and the Tiger Snake have been confirmed. Kreffts Tiger Snakes and Death Adders kept in captivity at Whyalla and subjected to normal seasonal and daily temperature fluctuations have also mated during autumn.

It is generally thought that in most species, the male seeks out the female during the mating season; but Rankin gives one account of a Black Snake mating in which it appears that the female sought out the male[21]. The male,

24

having been found, searched around for the female's tail and possibly bit it. He then twitched his body forward and emitted explosive hisses. The female was stretched out beneath the male. The male aligned his head behind hers and brought his tail up under hers. Copulation lasted about two minutes.

Peter Mirtschin has observed Taipans, Death Adders, and Kreffts Tiger Snakes mating and they all follow similar patterns. The male follows the female around and positions his body on top of hers. The male rubs his head on the female's neck and at the same time imposes jerking pressure on her. The male's tail is very active during this period. It rubs on and beside the female's tail in waves of fast and slow vibrations. Males seem to be stimulated by females during a period from just before a skin slough to just after. In fact, some keepers use this knowledge to induce breeding by rubbing the sloughed skin of another snake on to the female. Sexual maturation in females occurs at twenty-four months in Copperheads and Tiger Snakes and at about thirty-one months for Red-bellied Black Snakes[22]. Males mature at slightly younger ages than females. Death Adders born at Whyalla showed mating activity nineteen months after birth. (See photograph, page 37.)

The Australian dangerously venomous snakes are either oviparous (egg laying) or ovoviviparous (producing eggs which hatch within the female). With the exception of the Taipan, the Brown Snakes, Colletts Snake, the Spotted Black Snake, some races of the Mulga Snake, and the Black Whip Snake, all other snakes described in this book are ovoviviparous. (See photographs, pages 37 and 38.)

Oviparous snakes deposit their eggs under logs, rocks, or debris and in so doing subject the eggs to the risk of dehydration, predation, or thermal shock. A gravid female ovoviviparous snake carries the developing snakes inside her oviducts and therefore if she dies for any reason, all juvenile snakes die with her.

Hibernation

Of the dangerously venomous snakes, only the southern

25

snakes go through a period of relative inactivity. In winter they seek refuge from the cold weather but will come out to bask (see Glossary) on sunny days. On Eyre Peninsula, King Brown Snakes that are generally dark in colour have been noted on a number of occasions basking in the winter sun, their dark colour enabling greater radiation absorption.

Growth

Shine (1978) records that Tiger Snakes, Red-bellied Black Snakes, and Copperheads more than double their length in their first year[22]. Peter Mirtschin found that in captivity it is possible to increase Death Adders' birth weight thirty times in their first year of life. Wild Death Adders would not be expected to grow so quickly. Young snakes grow quickly and consequently skin sloughs are much more frequent early in a snake's life.

Elimination

Yellowy-white uric acid from the kidneys passes via the ureters to the cloaca and is excreted with the intestinal wastes. Snakes have no bladder and little urine is excreted. After excretion the waste bolus dries and the uric acid forms a white powder.

Head morphology

The teeth are sharp, needle-like, and recurved. They form three groups. On the lower jaw, the dentary bone houses the mandibular teeth used for gripping the prey and drawing it into the mouth. On the upper jaw the maxillary bone carries the maxillary teeth, fang, and reserve fangs. The fangs, enclosed in a fleshy sheath called the *vagina dentis*, are used to inject venom hyperdermically to immobilise the prey. The maxillary teeth are used for clasping the prey. The fangs are capable of very small degrees of rotation depending on the snake, with the Death Adder exhibiting more than any other of the Australian snakes. This degree of rotation does not match that of the Vipers from the Americas, Africa, Asia, and Europe. In Vipers, fangs that are highly elevated by rotation represent a far more efficient biting mechanism than the relatively fixed fangs of Australian snakes. This is because the angle of entry into the biting surface is less acute or more direct with rotated fangs than with fixed fangs. Australian snakes make up for their poor venom delivery system with highly toxic venoms.

With elapid snakes, the fangs remain relatively fixed when the snake closes its mouth, but in Vipers the fangs rotate or fold back. In the frequent struggles with prey, fangs are sometimes lost, and these are quickly replaced by reserve fangs which then become fully functional.

Poison is transmitted from the poison gland behind the eye, passes through the poison duct and through the grooved fang which is effectively hollow. (See photograph, page 39.) Because of the anatomical attachments of the anterior temporal muscle to the mandible and its relationship to the venom gland, the bitten part must be firmly gripped with both jaws for an effective bite. An exception to this may occur when the venom glands are full and some of their contents may be ejected under pressure of a snap bite[1].

The palatine bone carries the palatine teeth, used for gripping and swallowing.

The trachea (wind-pipe) is positioned forward in the bottom jaw and allows the snake to breathe while eating prey larger than its head.

Chapter 3

IDENTIFICATION OF DANGEROUS TERRESTRIAL SNAKES

All snakes reviewed in this book are capable of inflicting a serious or lethal bite. Identification involves handling the snake, so lay persons should not attempt to identify any snake unless it is definitely dead.

Identification entails searching through the colour photographs in the book until a snake of similar colour is found, then comparing the scalation count and head scales.

If no similar colour photograph is present, check the scalation with Table 3.1 (p. 30). When a match is found, check the head pattern of the snake on the appropriate page.

The scale counting technique is shown in Diagram 6 (p. 31). Head scale nomenclature is shown in Diagrams 3 and 4, but it is not necessary to know these for identification. Simply compare orientation and size. Diagram 5 shows keeled scales.

These techniques should help you at least to put the snake into the correct genus.

In your identification attempts it is possible that colour variations not covered by the book will occur. In addition, you may also find and identify snakes outside the ranges shown on the distribution maps. In either case, your local museum would be glad to receive such information; or better still, the specimen.

Facing page:
Diagrams 3 and 4
Head scale nomenclature
Diagram 5
Keeled scales of the Desert Death Adder Acanthophis pyrrhus

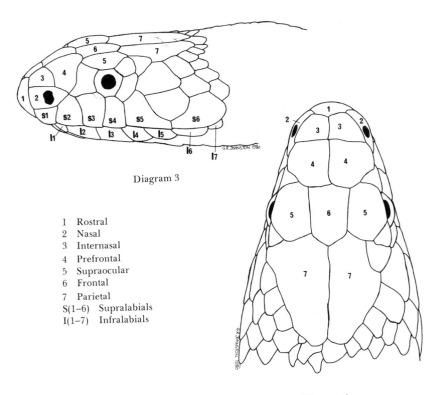

Diagram 3

1 Rostral
2 Nasal
3 Internasal
4 Prefrontal
5 Supraocular
6 Frontal
7 Parietal
S(1–6) Supralabials
I(1–7) Infralabials

Diagram 4

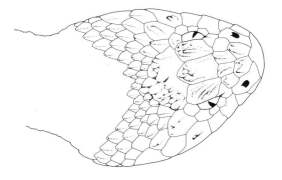

Diagram 5

29

Snake	Ventrals	Subcaudals	Anal	Mid-bodies
Common Tiger	140–190	35–65 single	single	17 or 19
Kreffts Tiger	163–173	41–50 single	single	17
Peninsula Tiger	160–184	45–54 single	single	17, 18, 19, 21
Western Tiger	140–165	36–51 single	single	17, 19
Chappell Is. Tiger	160–171	47–52 single	single	17
Tasmanian and King Is. Tiger	161–174	48–53 single	single	17, 15
Common Brown	185–235	45–75 divided	divided	17
Peninsula Brown	190–205	52–62 divided	divided	17
Western Brown	180–230	50–70 divided	divided	17 or 19
Speckled Brown	190–220	44–70 divided	divided	19 to 21
Dugite	190–230	50–70 divided	divided	19
Tanners Brown	190–230	50–70 divided	divided	19
Ingrams Brown	190–220	55–70 divided	divided	17
Taipan	220–250	45–80 divided	single	21–23
Inland Taipan	211–250	52–70 divided	single	23
Death Adder	110–130	38–55 mostly single	single	21–23
Desert Death Adder	140–160	45–60 single anterior, divided posterior 47–57	single	21
Northern Death Adder	122–134	19–39 single 14–29 paired	single	21, 23
Red-bellied Black	180–210	40–65 first $1/3$ single, rest divided	divided	17
Mulga	189–220	53–70 all single or all divided or partly single and divided	divided	17
Colletts	215–235	50–70 single anterior, divided posterior	divided	19
Spotted Black	175–205	45–65 single anterior, divided posterior	divided	19
Butlers Snake	204–216	55–65	divided	17
Copperhead	140–165	35–55 single	single	15, 13, 17
Stephens Banded	220–250	50–70 single	single	21
Broad-headed	200–230	40–65 single	single	21
Pale-headed	190–225	40–65 single	single	19 or 21
Rough-scaled	160–185	50–60 single	single	23
Small-eyed	165–210	30–46 single	single	15
Black Whip	160–220	70–105 paired	divided	15

Table 3.1 *Scalation summary of dangerous snakes*

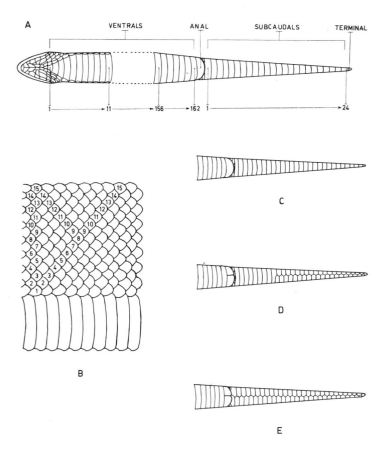

Diagram 6 *Scale counting technique* (reproduced with permission from P. A. Rawlinson and the *Victorian Naturalist*).

A Ventral aspect of an elapid snake with scale terminology.

B Skin removed from mid-body of a snake and spread out to show the method of making mid-body scale counts.

C Ventral aspect of an elapid snake tail showing single anal scale and sub-caudal scales.

D Ventral aspect showing divided anal scale and subcaudals single anterior, divided posterior.

E Ventral aspect showing divided anal scale and divided subcaudals.

If you are unable to identify the snake using this book, it is possible that the specimen is either:

- A harmless snake, such as a Python, or Tree Snake.
- A venomous snake not considered dangerous.
- A legless lizard.
- An undescribed, new species of snake.
- A snake described by this book but having scale counts outside the known range.

See photographs, pages 39 to 41.

Top: Variegated Gecko *Gehyra variegata. Bottom:* Bearded Dragon *Amphibolurus vitticeps.* (See page 19.)

Top: Painted Dragon *Amphibolurus pictus*. *Bottom:* Mountain Devil *Moloch horridus*. (See page 19.)

34

Top: Death Adder devouring a mouse. *Bottom:* Common Brown Snake constrict-ing and biting its prey. (See page 21.)

Top: The milky eyes of a Peninsula Tiger Snake prior to shedding its skin. *Bottom left:* Ventral surface of Kreffts Tiger Snake, showing mucus-like secretions beneath the skin prior to shedding. *Bottom right:* Death Adder shedding skin. (See pages 23 to 24.)

Top left: Common Brown Snake hemipenes.
(See page 24.) *Top right:* Death Adders
mating. *Bottom left:* Taipan laying eggs.
Bottom right: Common Brown Snake hatching
from an egg. (See page 25.)

Left: Eggs of Colletts Snake hatching. (Photograph by B. Barnett.) *Below:* Juvenile Death Adders are born live. *Bottom:* Death Adder emerging from transparent embryo sac. (See page 25.)

Below: Blind snake *Typhlina bituberculata* (harmless). (See page 32.) *Right:* Fang of a Kangaroo Island Tiger Snake. (Photograph by Dr D. Henderson.) (See page 27.) *Bottom:* Children's python *Liasis childreni* (harmless). (See page 32.)

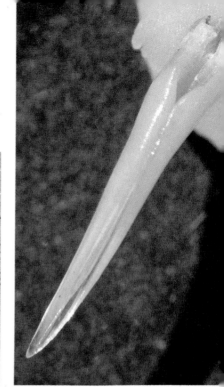

Far left: Half-girdled Snake *Simoselaps semifasciatus* (venomous but not dangerous). *Left:* Burtons Lizard *Lialis burtonis.* *Bottom left:* Common Scaly-foot Lizard *Pygopus lepidopodus. Bottom centre:* Legless Lizard *Delma nasuta. Below:* Pretty legless lizard *Aprasia* sp. (All harmless—see page 32.)

41

Top: Common Tiger Snake, albino. *Bottom:* Common Tiger Snake—Kangaroo Island. (See pages 82 to 84.)

Top and bottom: Common Tiger Snakes showing variation in colour. (See pages 82 to 84.)

43

Top and bottom: Common Tiger Snakes showing variation in colour. (See pages 82 to 84.)

44

Top: Common Tiger Snake, faintly banded. *Bottom:* Common Tiger Snake, un-banded. (See pages 82 to 84.)

45

Top: Kreffts Tiger Snake, banded. *Centre:* Kreffts Tiger Snake. *Bottom:* Kreffts Tiger Snake, juvenile. (See pages 84 to 87.) *Top right:* Peninsula Tiger Snake—Coffin Bay. *Centre right:* Peninsula Tiger Snake—Kangaroo Island. *Bottom right:* Peninsula Tiger Snake—Reevesby Island (juvenile). (See pages 87 to 91.)

46

Top and bottom: Western Tiger Snakes. (See pages 91 to 93.)

48

Top and bottom: Chappell Island Tiger Snakes. (See pages 93 to 95.)

49

Top left and right: King Island Tiger Snakes. *Centre:* Tasmanian Tiger Snake.
Bottom: Tasmanian Tiger Snake, juvenile. (See pages 95 to 97.)

50

Top: Tasmanian Tiger Snake, juvenile. *Bottom:* Tasmanian Tiger Snake. (See pages 95 to 97.)

Top and bottom: Common Brown Snakes showing variation in colour. (See pages 98 to 100.)

Top: Common Brown Snake. *Bottom:* Common Brown Snakes from Renmark, South Australia, showing variation in colour. (See pages 98 to 100.)

Top and bottom: Peninsula Brown Snakes, showing variation in colour. (See pages 100 to 103.)

Top and bottom: Peninsula Brown Snakes, showing variation in colour. (See pages 100 to 103.)

Six Western Brown Snakes, showing considerable variation in colour. (See pages 103 to 105.)

Top and bottom: Speckled Brown Snakes. (See pages 105 to 106.)
(Bottom photograph by M. Gillam)

58

Top and bottom: Dugites. (See pages 106 to 108.)

59

Top left: Tanners Brown Snake—Rottnest Island. (Photograph by S. Wilson.) (See pages 108 to 109.) *Bottom left:* Ingrams Brown Snake. (See pages 109 to 111.) *Top right and centre right:* Taipan, juvenile. *Below:* Head of Taipan. (See pages 111 to 113.)

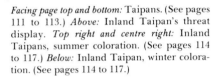

Facing page top and bottom: Taipans. (See pages 111 to 113.) *Above:* Inland Taipan's threat display. *Top right and centre right:* Inland Taipans, summer coloration. (See pages 114 to 117.) *Below:* Inland Taipan, winter coloration. (See pages 114 to 117.)

Top: Inland Taipan, winter coloration. (See pages 114 to 117.) *Bottom:* Northern Death Adder (Photo: Greg Harold). (See pages 122 to 123.)

64

Top right, centre right, and bottom: Common Death Adders—mallee. *Below:* Common Death Adder—coastal. (See pages 117 to 120.)

Top left: Common Death Adder—mallee. *Centre left:* Common Death Adder, juvenile—Sydney. *Bottom left:* Common Death Adder. *Top:* Head of Northern Death Adder. *Bottom:* Head of Common Death Adder—southern. (See pages 117 to 120.)

Top: Desert Death Adder. (See pages 120 to 122.) *Bottom:* Red-bellied Black Snake. (See pages 124 to 126.)

68

Top and bottom: Mulga Snakes. (See pages 126 to 128.)

Top: Mulga Snake. (See pages 126 to 128.) *Bottom:* Butlers Snake (Photo: Steve Wilson). (See pages 132 to 134.) *Facing page, top and centre:* Colletts Snakes. *Bottom:* Colletts Snake, juvenile. (See pages 128 to 130.)

Top and bottom: Spotted Black Snakes. (See pages 130 to 132.)

Top and bottom: Lowland Copperheads. (See pages 134 to 137.)

73

Top left: Lowland Copperhead. *Top right:* Highland Copperhead. *Bottom:* Pygmy Copperhead. (See pages 134 to 137.) *Facing page, top:* Pale-headed Snake. (See pages 138 to 139.) *Facing page, bottom:* Stephens Banded Snake. (See pages 139 to 141.)

Top left and centre left: Broad-headed Snake. (See pages 141 to 143.) *Centre right:* Rough-scaled Snake. (See pages 143 to 145.) *Bottom:* Small-eyed Snake. (See pages 145 to 147.)

Top: Black Whip Snake. (See pages 147 to 148.) *Bottom:* Devastation of habitat of Death Adders, Black Tiger Snakes, and Peninsula Brown Snakes on lower Eyre Peninsula, South Australia. (See page 150.)

Top left: Clearing Boxthorn bushes from Winceby Island. (See page 153.) *Top right:* Boxes for housing the Common Death Adder juveniles. *Bottom:* Deformed Death Adder. (See page 160.)

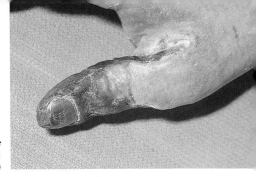

Top right: An extreme outcome showing necrosis resulting from a Mulga Snake bite (Photo: J. White). *Centre left:* Black Snake bite on finger (Photo: J. White). *Centre right:* Incised snake bite. (See page 165.) *Bottom:* Resuscitation of a snake-bite victim: note intravenous line, anaesthetic machine, oxygen therapy. (See page 173.)

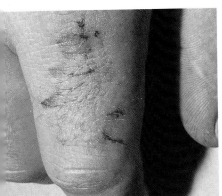

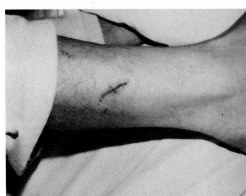

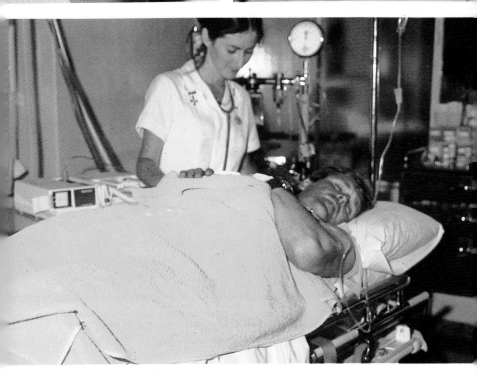

Top: Milking a Reevesby Island Tiger Snake by the conventional method, in which the snake bites through a stretched rubber membrane. *Bottom:* The plastic pipette method of milking (Reevesby Island Tiger Snake). (See page 188.)

Chapter 4
THE SNAKES DESCRIBED

Notes on the genera

In the general discussion of each genus, reference to maximum and minimum temperature ranges should not be confused with preferred optimum temperatures of the snakes.

Maximum and minimum temperatures are used because they define meteorological areas and influence the weather and vegetation of areas. Snakes will usually be active or bask at temperatures within the average maximum and minimum extremes.

TIGER SNAKES

Storr[102] now includes *Austrelaps* in his concept of *Notechis*. Tiger Snakes (*Notechis*) have evolved to occupy the temperate-to-cool areas of Australia. Apart from the west coast of South Australia, parts of the Murray River and regions of Western Australia, they occur in localities where the average rainfall is greater than 500 mm.

Common Tiger Snakes (*N. scutatus*), Western Tiger Snakes (*N. ater occidentalis*) (mainland), Kreffts Tiger Snake (*N. ater ater*), and Tasmanian Tiger Snakes (*N. ater humphreysi*), feed mainly on frogs. The presence of water from either high rainfall or from river courses supplies the necessary dampness for frogs.

Maximum average summer temperatures throughout their range vary from 18°C in parts of Tasmania and Bass Strait to 31°C in the Flinders Ranges, South Australia, the Murray River area, and parts of Western Australia.

Two species of Tiger Snakes, divided into six main populations, are described here in the traditional way.

There are, however, enough ecological and venom differences among Tiger Snakes to recognise further variation. Electrophoretic patterns and toxicity experiments conducted by the Commonwealth Serum Laboratories have clearly illustrated great differences within species.

Tiger Snakes (*N. ater niger*) found on the small archipelago of the Sir Joseph Banks Group in Spencer Gulf, show ecological variations among the different island populations. The Tiger Snakes on Reevesby Island are large and feed mainly on the White-faced Storm-Petrel[6, 23]. The Tiger Snakes are much smaller on nearby Roxby Island. Here they appear to feed mainly on small birds and skinks, since Storm-Petrels do not appear to occur on Roxby Island. On Hopkins Island, the Tiger Snakes are larger than those on Reevesby Island. Tiger Snakes on Hopkins Island feed on Muttonbirds and those on Hareby appear to feed on Storm-Petrels[24].

COMMON TIGER SNAKE *Notechis scutatus* (Peters)

Description Flat blunt head, slightly distinct from a robust body. Body capable of being flattened along entire length when snake is agitated or when basking.

Average length 0·9 m, maximum about 1·2 m; but has been recorded at 2 m[25].

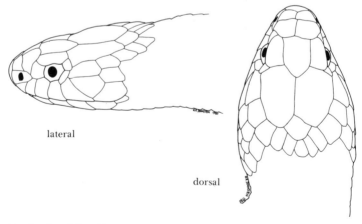

lateral

dorsal

Head scales of *Notechis scutatus*

Scalation   Scales appear like overlapping shields, especially around the neck.

VENTRALS	140–190
SUBCAUDALS	35–65 all single
MIDBODIES	17 or 19 rows
ANAL	single

Colour   Highly variable. Base colours are brown, grey, olive, green with lighter crossbands usually of a creamy yellow colour. Occasionally unbanded Tiger Snakes are found. (See photographs, pages 42 to 45.)

Habits   The ecology of Tiger Snakes revolves around the availability of frogs or tadpoles. Although adult Tiger Snakes have adapted well to survive on introduced mice (*Mus musculus*), the juveniles require small frogs or tadpoles for food.

Tiger snakes are ovoviviparous producing about 35 young but up to 80 have been recorded in a single brood[7].

Habitat and distribution   Tiger Snakes always occur in well-watered areas where frogs can be found; this restricts them to watercourses, swamps, lakes, or wet mountain slopes.

Venom $LD_{50} = 0 \cdot 118^2$ Yield   35 mg[2]
Strongly neurotoxic and coagulant[26]. Weakly haemolytic and cytotoxic[26]. Some myotoxin present[14].
Specific antivenom   Tiger Snake[26]
Initial dose of antivenom   3000 units[26]

Special features   Although the Tiger Snake is still common in many areas, its overall numbers have been reduced drastically. The main reason for this reduction is habitat alteration. For example, river level control along the Murray River has reduced annual flooding patterns. This has altered the water table and reduced the numbers of swamps and lagoons[8]. In south-western Victoria, the extensive stone walls, once a haven for snakes, have been replaced by wire fences. Lakes and swamps in many areas have been drained for farming purposes. In some developed areas there are now reduced but balanced Tiger Snake populations. For instance, Tiger Snakes are occasionally found in Sydney or Melbourne along watercourses or golf courses. Tiger Snakes are still abundant in Altona, a Melbourne suburb. Fortunately Tiger Snakes are well represented in National Parks.

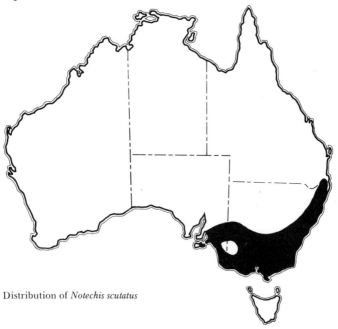

Distribution of *Notechis scutatus*

Food   Predominantly frogs and tadpoles, especially in their natural state, but in man-changed environments, which applies nearly everywhere today, they thrive on introduced mice *Mus musculus*. Other animals eaten are lizards, birds, rats, eels, and fish[25]. Tiger Snakes, because of their association with water, are highly prone to trematode or fluke infestation. These flukes are transmitted by frogs and water snails and appear to be causing problems in certain areas[27].

KREFFTS TIGER SNAKE *Notechis ater ater* (Krefft)

Description   Robust in appearance with a broad flat head which is slightly distinct from body. Average length about 83 cm.

84

Scalation   Smooth scales. Appear like overlapping shields around neck.

VENTRALS	163–173
SUBCAUDALS	41–50[17] all single
MIDBODIES	17 rows
ANAL	single (occasionally divided)[28]

Colour   Seventy per cent of specimens have either distinct yellow-white bands or remnant banding. The remainder are jet black. Many specimens exhibit white markings around the bottom jaw. Juvenile possess white bands. The ventral surface is dark grey to black tending to creamish before sloughing. (See photographs, page 46.)

Habits   These snakes can be found basking in relatively cold weather, their black colour optimising radiation absorption. In the hot weather they become aquatic and live exclusively around permanent water where they feed on tadpoles and frogs. They can be seen muzzling under submerged flat rocks in search of tadpoles. Ovoviviparous — produces 6 to 15 young[29].

Habitat and distribution   Their range is restricted to a narrow corridor of the Flinders Ranges, from Wilmington to Melrose, in the approximate confines of the 600 mm

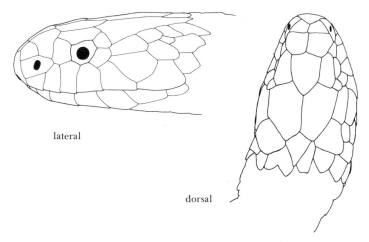

lateral

dorsal

Head scales of *Notechis ater ater*

average annual isohyet. The area is typified by deep-gullied gorges, carved out by creeks dotted with River Red Gums. In summer the creeks form a series of ponds that are ideal for frogs and tadpoles.

The dependence on tadpoles and frogs by the juvenile snakes restricts the Kreffts Tiger Snake to this wetter habitat, despite the ability of the adult snakes to feed on mice.

Kreffts Tiger Snakes occur in Mt Remarkable National Park.

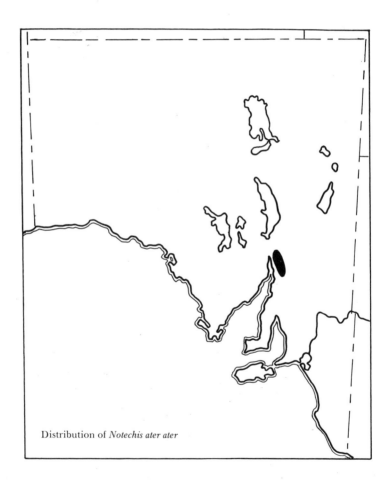

Distribution of *Notechis ater ater*

Venom Yield 23 mg[9]
Preliminary work on this snake's venom has indicated that it is more toxic than that of the Common Tiger Snake[30]. The effect of the venom on laboratory animals clearly demonstrates that it is highly venomous.
Specific antivenom Tiger Snake
Initial dose of antivenom 3000 units

Special features The snake's black colour is intriguing. One theory is that radiation absorption is limited in the steep-gullied areas of its range and black helps optimise it. Moreover, the creeks containing tadpoles and frogs are relatively cool and the snakes are continually in and out of the water seeking to re-elevate their temperatures. In winter snakes travel away from water and have been recorded basking on top of Mt Remarkable on warm days.
Food In its natural state, frogs, tadpoles and lizards are the main food source. European mice *Mus musculus* are also favoured. These snakes have also been observed feeding on ducklings of *Anas supercilosa* (Black Duck).

PENINSULA TIGER SNAKE *Notechis ater niger* (Kinghorn)

Description Robust in appearance. Average length 1·1 m. Roxby Island snakes average 86 cm in length. Blunt head slightly distinct from body. The Kangaroo Island Tiger Snake specimens have fang lengths of about 5 mm[31].

Scalation Smooth scales. Appear like overlapping shields around the neck.

VENTRALS	160–184
SUBCAUDALS	45–54 all single
MIDBODIES	17, 18, 19, rarely 21[28, 32]
ANAL	Single

Colour Generally jet black, with adults occasionally possessing white markings around the bottom jaw. Juveniles nearly always have white cross bands. On Kangaroo Island banding often occurs in adult specimens. Ventral surface dark grey to black tending to cream before sloughing. (See photographs, page 47.)

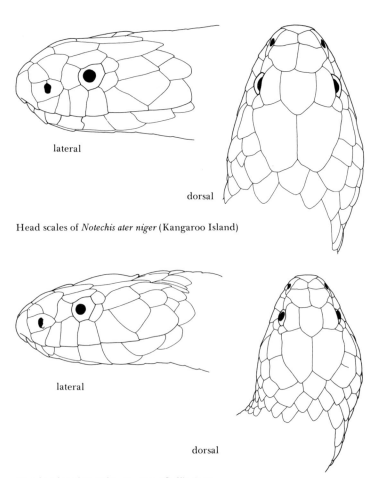

lateral

dorsal

Head scales of *Notechis ater niger* (Kangaroo Island)

lateral

dorsal

Head scales of *Notechis ater niger* (Coffin Bay)

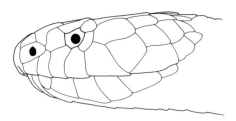

Head scales of *Notechis ater niger* (Hopkins Island)

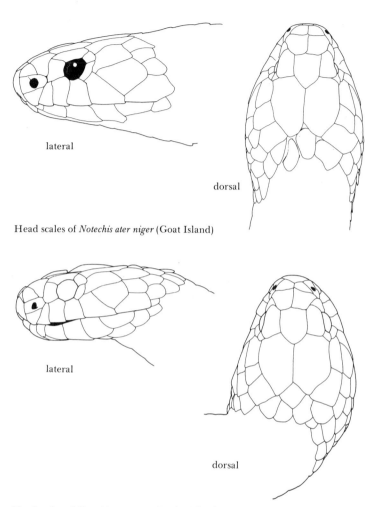

lateral

dorsal

Head scales of *Notechis ater niger* (Goat Island)

lateral

dorsal

Head scales of *Notechis ater niger* (Roxby Island)

Habits Ovoviviparous producing up to 20 live young. The black coloration presumably allows the snake to bask more efficiently during the warmer winter days. Usually far more sluggish than the Common Tiger Snake and less vigorous when caught.

Habitat and distribution Occurs on the offshore islands in Spencer Gulf, Kangaroo Island, the west coast of South

Australia, and coastal sand dunes of lower Eyre Peninsula and Yorke Peninsula. Vegetation consists of coastal dunes with low shrubs, low eucalypt woodlands to eucalypt forests on Kangaroo Island. Some small islands have samphire and saltbush communities.

Venom $LD_{50} = 0.099$[2]   Yield 34.3 mg[6]
The Peninsula Tiger Snake possesses the most toxic venom of all the Tiger Snake groups.
Specific antivenom Tiger Snake[33]
Initial dose of antivenom 3000 units[33]

Special features Fishermen living in the Tumby Bay area have reported Tiger Snakes swimming in the sea up to 10 km from land. This suggests they occasionally commute from island to island in the Sir Joseph Banks Group and also from the islands to the mainland. However, apparent ecological and size differences between populations seem to discount this possibility.

The black coloration is a source of interest and wonder. One explanation is that Tiger Snakes from this area are black so that optimum use of radiation can be obtained. However, good basking weather is more readily available in these habitats than, say, in Mount Gambier, where ordinary banded Common Tiger Snakes occur. Another explanation for the black colour is that it aids in more rapid digestion of food (quicker radiation absorption is required to elevate the body temperature to its optimum level for food digestion) thus allowing the snake to eat more in a shorter time span. Black would hardly be expected to provide much camouflage on white sand dunes, but at a glance a black snake could be taken as a shadow. Generally speaking the island Tiger Snakes are less aggressive in nature than the Common Tiger Snake, especially the larger ones. In the cooler weather they have been known to lie coiled up and remain motionless when approached. Freshly caught specimens appear to be less perturbed about being caught than other snakes.

Food Adult island snakes mainly feed on birds such as White-faced Storm-Petrels (*Pelagodroma marina*) and Muttonbirds (*Puffinus tenuirostris*). Occasionally other birds

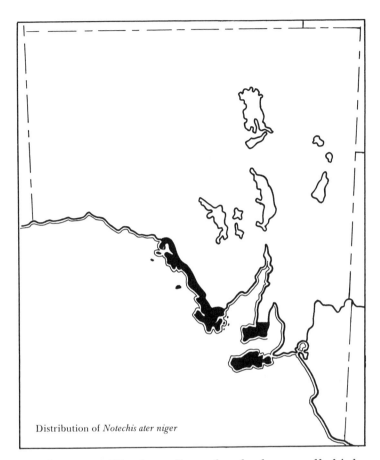

Distribution of *Notechis ater niger*

are also eaten. The juvenile snakes feed on small skinks. Mice have been introduced by man's inhabitation or farming activities, and these have provided another food source. On the mainland, birds and small mammals are eaten by these snakes.

WESTERN TIGER SNAKE *Notechis ater occidentalis* (Glauert) (Storr[102] suggests *N. scutatus occidentalis*)

Description   Broad short head slightly distinct from body. Robust body. Maximum length about 2 m.

Scalation   Smooth scales.
    VENTRALS   140–165[102]

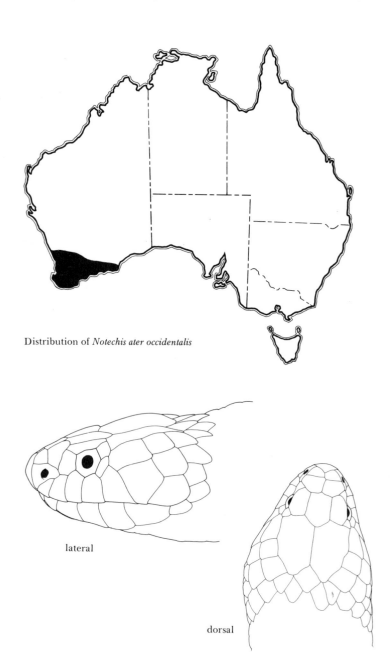

Distribution of *Notechis ater occidentalis*

lateral

dorsal

Head scales of *Notechis ater occidentalis*

92

SUBCAUDALS	36–51[102] all single
MIDBODIES	17, 19[102]
ANAL	Single (rarely divided[102])

Colour Steel blue to black with bright yellow bands. Ventral surface yellow tending to black towards the tail. All-black specimens are common. (See photographs, page 48.)

Habits Ovoviviparous producing up to 90 young[8]. Gow records young at 15 cm from litters of 14 to 20[25]. Observations on Carnac Island suggest a mortality rate of 90 per cent in the first 6 months. Lifespan has been measured at over 10 years[8].

Habitat and distribution South-western Western Australia and some adjacent islands including Garden and Carnac. Frogs abound in the forests and swamps in the region. Dry sclerophyll forest.

Venom $LD_{50} = 0.124$[2] Yield 35 mg[8]
Specific antivenom Tiger Snake
Initial dose of antivenom 3000 units

CHAPPELL ISLAND TIGER SNAKE *Notechis ater serventyi* (Worrell)

Description Giant race of Tiger Snakes averaging about 1·9 m. Head slightly distinct from neck. Robust snake. (See photographs, page 49.)

Scalation Smooth scales.
VENTRALS	160–171
SUBCAUDALS	47–52 all single
MIDBODIES	17
ANAL	Single

Colour Dorsum olive brown to black. Ventral surface is usually lighter in colour. Juveniles may be banded.

Habits Generally sluggish. Specimens from Chappell Island are easily kept in captivity and fed on a variety of foods such as mice, rats, strips of meat, and sausages[7]. Ovoviviparous; 6–20 young measuring 25–30 cm.

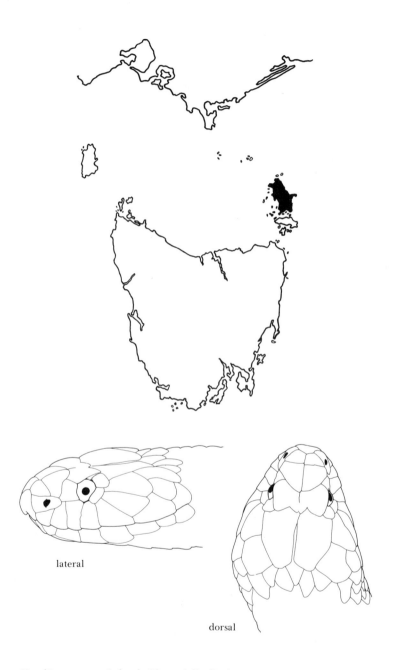

Notechis ater serventyi— head scales and distribution

Habitat and distribution   Occurs on Chappell Island and Badger Island of the Furneaux group. Lives in Muttonbird burrows where it finds refuge and feeds on juvenile Muttonbirds *Puffinus tenuirostris*. Also found on Flinders Island, Cat, Babel, Forsyth, and Vansittart islands.

We have lumped the Furneaux group Tiger Snakes into *N. ater serventyi* purely on the basis of island proximity. Insufficient information is available to do otherwise at this stage.

Venom $LD_{50} = 0 \cdot 271$[2]   Average yield 75 mg[7]
Specific antivenom   Tiger Snake[26]
Initial dose of antivenom   12 000 units[26]

Special features   Most of the work in understanding the ecology of this snake has been compiled by E. Worrell[7, 34]. He records that on Chappell Island, these Tiger Snakes feed on young Muttonbirds for several weeks and virtually starve for the rest of the year. The juveniles feed on small skinks.

TASMANIAN AND KING ISLAND TIGER SNAKES
Notechis ater humphreysi (Worrell)

Description   Large adults are robust with broad blunt

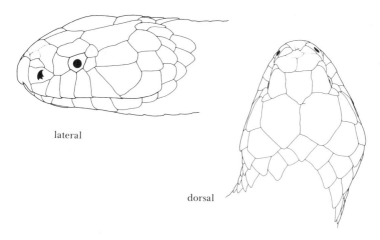

lateral

dorsal

Head scales of *Notechis ater humphreysi* (King Island)

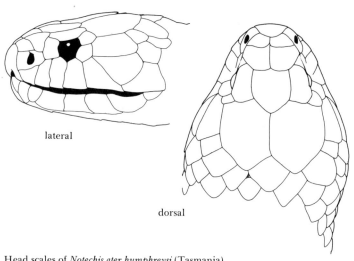

lateral

dorsal

Head scales of *Notechis ater humphreysi* (Tasmania)

heads. Younger snakes are slimmer and similar to other
Tiger Snakes. Maximum length about 1·5 m[25]

Scalation   Smooth scales.

VENTRALS	161–174
SUBCAUDALS	48–53 all single
MIDBODIES	17 (sometimes 15). Worrell records that mid-body scales may count between 15 and 19 on the same snake.
ANAL	Single[7]

Colour   Grey with black flecks which form faint bands;
black; black with yellow stripes. Ventral surface usually
lighter in colour. (See photographs, pages 50 and 51.)

Habits   On Christmas and New Year islands they feed on
Muttonbird chicks. King Island Tiger Snakes have cannibalistic tendencies. Ovoviviparous and produces large
numbers of young[7].

Habitat and distribution   Sclerophyll forest, woodlands,
heathland, and rainforest occur on King Island, Tasmania,
Seal Rocks, Christmas Island, New Year Island, and Bruny
Island.

Distribution of *Notechis ater humphreysi*

Venom   Worrell records that the King Island Tiger Snake is less toxic than other Tiger Snakes. Victims bitten by Tasmanian Tiger Snakes, on average, require twice the usual dose of antivenom for the Common Tiger Snake.
Specific antivenom   Tiger Snake[26]
Initial dose of antivenom   6000 units[26]

THE BROWN SNAKES

The Brown Snakes (genus *Pseudonaja*) are a group of snakes exhibiting similar scalation, hooded threat display (false cobra), and methods of prey restraint.

In addition to using their venom to kill their prey, Brown Snakes also constrict. The prey then either dies from the action of the venom or by suffocation. Constriction is a technique primarily used by pythons and boas for

97

hunting and its main effect is to stop the prey from breathing. Tight coils around the prey prevent chest expansion necessary for air intake, and so the prey dies of suffocation. Brown Snakes using this technique either use it to supplement the action of the venom or to prevent the prey from biting while struggling to escape.

Pseudonaja modesta, a non-dangerous but venomous Brown Snake, does not use this technique of prey restraint[35].

Brown Snakes occur over the entire mainland of Australia occupying almost all types of environments and habitats. Generally speaking they are fast-moving and sun-loving snakes preferring higher temperature ranges of activity.

The taxonomy of Brown Snakes has been incomplete for quite some time. For instance, Ingrams Brown Snake *P. ingrami* is not regarded as a valid species by some taxonomists who synonymise it with the Common Brown Snake *P. textilis textilis* on the basis of scalation. The Dugite *P. affinis affinis* and Peninsula Brown Snake *P. textilis inframacula* could also be closely associated.

The Brown Snakes occur in all rainfall areas with the Dugite and the Peninsula Brown Snake occupying almost identical thermal regions with average maximum summer temperatures of 24°C–32°C.

The more southern and coastal Brown Snakes tend to be smaller and darker in colour, which may have some radiation absorption advantages.

With the exception of the top end of the Northern Territory, Western Brown Snakes tend to occupy the more arid parts of Australia, having an average maximum temperature range of 30°C–39°C, and similar rainfalls.

COMMON BROWN SNAKE *Pseudonaja textilis textilis* (Dume'ril and Bibron)

Description Long and slender, head not distinct from body, juveniles often banded or with black heads. Can grow to more than 1·8 m. Generally southern Brown Snakes do not grow to as great a length as northern specimens. Buchal cavity flesh pink for Northern Territory specimens[35].

Scalation   Smooth scales.
VENTRALS   185–235
SUBCAUDALS   45–75 divided
MIDBODIES   17
ANAL   Divided

Colour   Variable in colour but usually a monotone brown. Juveniles can be banded. Light tan to dark brown. Ventral surfaces often blotched with orange, grey, or brown spots. (See photographs, pages 52 and 53.)

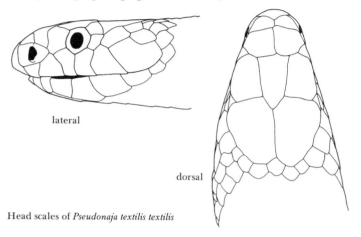

lateral

dorsal

Head scales of *Pseudonaja textilis textilis*

Habits   Oviparous producing about 10–30 eggs. Extremely fast-moving, alert, and very difficult to catch. Of all the Brown Snakes, the Common Brown Snake probably retaliates the most vigorously when threatened. Brown Snakes usually like slightly warmer weather than most other snakes and are mainly diurnal.

Habitat and distribution   Found in a range of habitats, from dry areas to watercourse swamps, and have adapted to man-made changes to the environment. Brown Snakes are common in farmlands of the eastern States.

Venom $LD_{50} = 0.041$[2]   Yield   2 mg[5]
Strong coagulant, neurotoxic, weakly haemolytic and cyto-

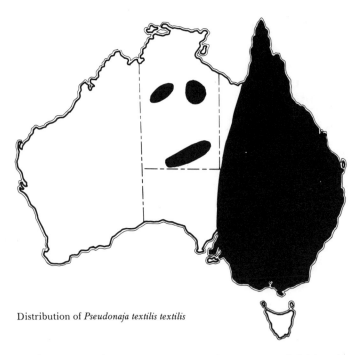

Distribution of *Pseudonaja textilis textilis*

toxic. Myotoxin is present. 2 mg is average yield but large specimens up to 2·1 m have yielded over 40 mg[7].
Specific antivenom　Brown Snake[26]
Initial dose of antivenom　1000 units[26]

Special features　*Food*　Essentially Brown Snakes prefer small lizards and frogs but have learnt to be extremely efficient hunters of introduced mice *Mus musculus*.

PENINSULA BROWN SNAKE　*Pseudonaja textilis inframacula* (Waite)

Description　Similar in shape to Common Brown Snake. Slender body, head indistinct from body.

Scalation

VENTRALS	190–205
SUBCAUDALS	52–62[28] divided
MIDBODIES	17 rows
ANAL	Divided

100

Colour Adult specimens range from light brown, dark brown, to almost black dorsally, with grey ventral surface. Darker spots are often scattered randomly along the dorsal surface. Juveniles are usually a light tan colour. (See photographs, pages 54 and 55.)

Habits Essentially a sun-loving snake, it is active in the warmer months except for days of extremely high temperature. Its dark colour enables it to be more active on cooler days than the Common Brown Snake and is probably an adaptation to the less favourable weather patterns of the more southern areas. On warm cloudy days it is not uncommon to find them basking, their dark colour optimising radiation absorption. Oviparous, producing 12–20 eggs.

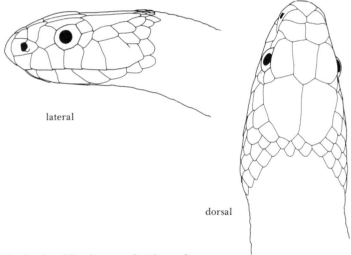

lateral

dorsal

Head scales of *Pseudonaja textilis inframacula*

Habitat and distribution Generally coastal dunes and coastal farmlands of southern Eyre Peninsula. It is found on Wardang Island. Not found more than 50 km from coastline. Very common in the Coffin Bay National Park.

Venom The Commonwealth Serum Laboratory is currently studying this venom. Until recently little has been known about the venom's toxicity although mice quickly

101

Distribution of *Pseudonaja textilis inframacula*

succumb following a bite. Peter Mirtschin was bitten by a Peninsula Brown Snake and suffered profound sweating accompanied by half an hour's breathing difficulty.

Specific antivenom   Brown Snake[33]
Initial dose of antivenom   1000 units[33]

Special features   Like other Brown Snakes, it has adapted well to man's environmental changes. In fact, adult specimens, while possibly less abundant in farmed areas than virgin areas, appear to grow larger and more robust and are less affected by tick parasites[28]. A contributory factor to their adaption would be the abundance of pest mice *Mus musculus* in these areas.

In temperament the Peninsula Brown Snake is usually a very quiet snake. It is quick to retreat when approached, and if caught, its adaption to captivity is rapid provided an acceptable food for each individual is supplied.

WESTERN BROWN SNAKE (Gwardar, Collared Brown Snake) *Pseudonaja nuchalis* (Gunther)

Description   Long slender snake, head indistinct from neck, head shorter than for Common Brown Snake. Buchal cavity bluish-black for Northern Territory specimens[35]. Iris red.

Scalation   Smooth scales, very shiny around head and neck. Rostral scale enlarged and strap-like; extends backwards slightly towards top of head. Head chisel-shaped when viewed from above.

VENTRALS	180–230
SUBCAUDALS	50–70 divided
MIDBODIES	17 or 19
ANAL	Divided

Colour   Colour is highly variable. Base colour varies from yellow to pitch black. Many specimens have black marking around head or neck. Banded individuals are not un-

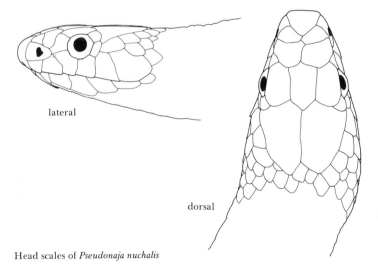

lateral

dorsal

Head scales of *Pseudonaja nuchalis*

103

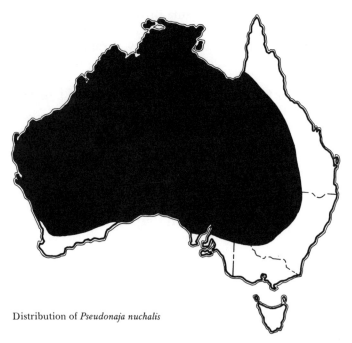

Distribution of *Pseudonaja nuchalis*

common. Most specimens have random spots over whole body. Seasonal colour changes in Western Brown Snakes have been recorded [103, 104]. They tend to change to lighter colours in warmer months. (See photographs, pages 56 and 57.)

Habits Fast-moving, alert, mostly diurnal but occasionally nocturnal. Prefers warmer weather. Lizards form the bulk of the diet, but European mice *Mus musculus* are now a favourite preference. Will occasionally eat small birds. Less vigorous than the Common Brown Snake when annoyed. Oviparous, laying about 20 eggs.

Habitat and distribution Lives in the drier parts of Australia and in tropical Northern Territory and part of Queensland.

Venom $LD_{50} = 0 \cdot 338^2$
The venom contains neurotoxic and haemolytic activity[25]. It is highly toxic to small mammals.

Specific antivenom   Brown Snake[33]
Initial dose of antivenom   1000 units[26]

Special features   Due to its wide distribution and its ability to adapt to changed environments it is probably one of Australia's most abundant snakes.
Food   In captivity they will feed on lizards, mice, rats, and birds.

SPECKLED BROWN SNAKE *Pseudonaja guttata* (Parker)

Description   Grows to about 1·4 m. Buchal cavity dark bluish[35]. (See photographs, page 58.)

Scalation   Smooth scales.
VENTRALS	190–220
SUBCAUDALS	44–70 divided
MIDBODIES	19–21
ANAL	Divided

Colour   Yellow or olive to apricot with black nicks to the sides of many of the dorsal scales. Some specimens possess dark broad bands. The ventral surface is from white to yellow which is blotched with orange[35].

Habits   A diurnal snake about which little is known[35].

Habitat and distribution   Restricted to blacksoil plains.

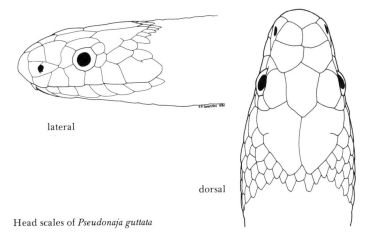

lateral

dorsal

Head scales of *Pseudonaja guttata*

105

Venom Yield 0·5 mg[10] Considered dangerous because of size but nothing is known of venom toxicity.
Specific antivenom Brown Snake
Initial dose of antivenom 1000 units

Distribution of *Pseudonaja guttata*

Special features M. Gillam records that 40% of specimens examined in the Northern Territory have had their tails missing[35]. (See *P. Ingrami* Ingrams Brown Snake, p. 109.) Threat attitude is a simple low arching of the neck in one bend with the section from the head to the bend being flattened. J. Bredl and B. Miller (pers. com.) have recorded a juvenile *P. guttata* being regurgitated by a Curl Snake *Suta suta.*
Food Captive specimens prefer lizards to mammals.

DUGITE   *Pseudonaja affinis affinis* (Gunther)

Description   Similar to the Western Brown Snake but has a rounded snout rather than the chisel-shaped rostral when viewed from above. Rostral not strap-like. Grows to 2 m. (See photographs, page 59.)

Scalation   Smooth scales.

VENTRALS	190–230
SUBCAUDALS	50–70 divided
MIDBODIES	19
ANAL	Divided

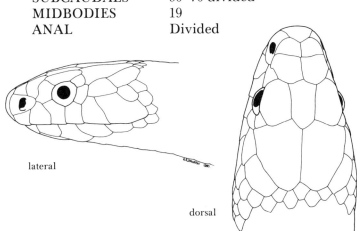

lateral

dorsal

Pseudonaja affinis affinis — head scales and distribution

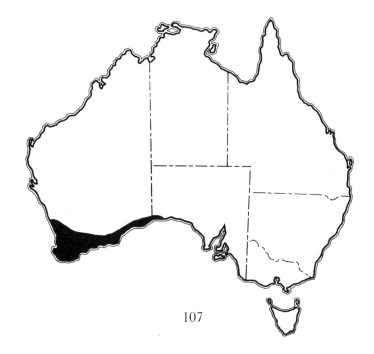

Colour   Dark brown, olive, tan usually liberally marked with irregular black scales. Ventral surface is greyish white[36].

Habits   Similar to other Brown Snakes. Oviparous with average clutch of 20 eggs[25, 36].

Habitat and distribution   Coastal southern Western Australia and into South Australia. Occurs in metropolitan area of Perth[36]. Dry sclerophyll and mallee.

Venom $LD_{50} = 0.56$[2]
A highly toxic venom.
Specific antivenom   Brown Snake [37]
Initial dose of antivenom   1000 units[26]

Special features   *Food*   Feeds on lizards and mice when they are available.

TANNERS BROWN SNAKE *Pseudonaja affinis tanneri* (Worrell)

Description   Grows to 1 m. (See photograph, page 60.)

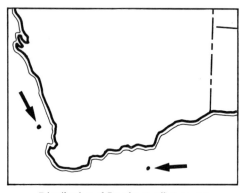

Distribution of *Pseudonaja affinis tanneri*

Scalation   Smooth scales
VENTRALS	190–230
SUBCAUDALS	50–70 divided
MIDBODIES	19
ANAL	Divided

108

Colour   Chestnut brown to black.

Habitat and distribution   Occurs on islands of Recherche Archipelago, south-west Western Australia. Specimens from Rottnest Island are for the time being included as this sub-species. Storr is currently investigating the Rottnest Island population (Western Australian Museum).

Habits   Unknown.

Venom   Unknown but considered to be dangerous because of the snake's size.
Specific antivenom   Brown Snake
Initial dose of antivenom   1000 units

INGRAMS   BROWN   SNAKE   *Pseudonaja   ingrami* (Boulenger)

Description   Some taxonomists have chosen to lump this population with *P. textilis textilis*. Buchal cavity predominantly black. Iris indistinct — entire eye appears to be black superficially. Largest specimen known 1·76 m[35]. (See photograph, page 60.)

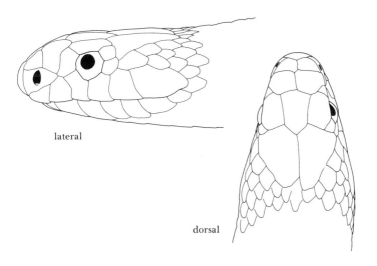

lateral

dorsal

Head scales of *Pseudonaja ingrami*

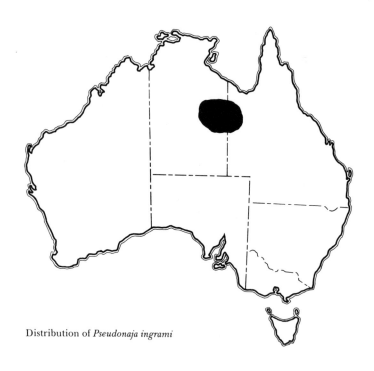

Distribution of *Pseudonaja ingrami*

Scalation   Smooth scales.

VENTRALS	190–220
SUBCAUDALS	55–70 divided
MIDBODIES	17
ANAL	Divided

Colour   Gillam lists 5 colour forms:
1. glossy black brown
2. dark brown anteriorly, golden brown posteriorly
3. uniform golden brown
4. head and nape grey brown to dark brown body light to rich yellow brown
5. pale olive brown.

Scales in all forms are darker at tips[35].

Habits   Diurnal. Preys predominantly on small mammals, mainly rats and mice, especially the long-haired rat *Rattus villosissimus* and European mouse *Mus musculus*[35].

Habitat and distribution   Seeks refuge in deep earth cracks. Blacksoil plains subject to seasonal flooding. Barkly Tableland.

Venom   Nothing known at this stage but assumed to be dangerous because of the snake's size.
Specific antivenom   Brown Snake
Initial dose of antivenom   1000 units

Special features   Activity mostly in early morning from 8 a.m. to 10.30 a.m. Gillam justifies species as distinct by iris colour, buchal cavity colour, and number of infralabials. 45% of specimens examined by Gillam had damaged tails or up to 10% missing. Gillam suggests this is due to predation as snakes leave their tails partially exposed after entering cracks in the ground[35].

TAIPANS

The Taipans (genus *Oxyuranus*) are the largest Australian dangerous snakes with long heads distinct from neck, slender necks, and distinguished from other snakes by scalation, dentition, hemipenis structure, and venom.

Two species occur in Australia and while some ecological similarities exist, their habitats and nature are totally different.

TAIPAN *Oxyuranus scutellatus scutellatus* (Peters)

Description   Large rectangular shaped head, narrow neck, cylindrical body and red eyes. Taipans have been recorded up to 2·8 m in length. (See photographs, pages 61 and 62.)

Scalation   Dorsal scales feebly keeled (especially on the neck and vertebral region) to smooth and small on the neck[38].

VENTRALS	220–250
SUBCAUDALS	45–80 divided
MIDBODIES	21–23
ANAL	Single

Colour   Taipans always exhibit a pale creamish colour around the head. The heads of juveniles are predomi-

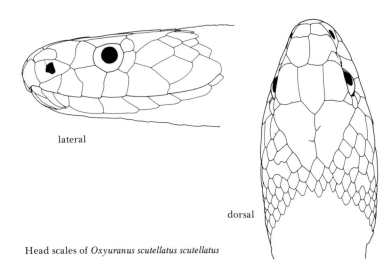

lateral

dorsal

Head scales of *Oxyuranus scutellatus scutellatus*

nantly pale, but the head darkens so that only the front remains pale in mature Taipans. Dorsally, Taipans have been recorded in colours of light brown, dark brown to black, coppery red, and olive. They have been recorded to undergo seasonal colour variation, changing to lighter colours during summer[103, 104].

Habits From observations in captivity, the Taipan is an efficient hunter, with a lightning fast strike, an acute sense of smell, and extremely alert eyesight. It moves rapidly in on its prey, strikes, retracts slightly, and waits for the venom to immobilise its victim, thus increasing its chance of success without injury to itself from the prey animal. Taipans are oviparous producing 7–20 eggs[38]. They occasionally lay 2 clutches of eggs in quick succession with less than 2 months between clutches[105].

Habitat and distribution The wetter coastal areas of Queensland, the Northern Territory, and Western Australia, with 800–1600 mm rainfall. Does not occur where average maximum winter temperature falls below 18°C. The Taipan prefers undulating country, but on Cape York Peninsula inhabits open woodland areas. Introduced lantana country is also a favoured habitat.

The sugar cane fields in Queensland abound with rats

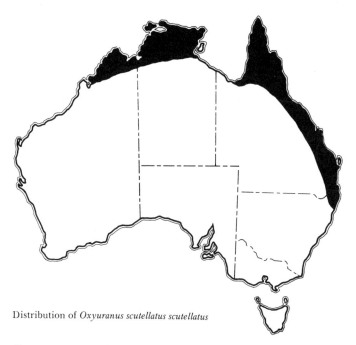

Distribution of *Oxyuranus scutellatus scutellatus*

Rattus rattus and *Melomys* spp which provide an excellent food source[39].

Venom $LD_{50} = 0.064$[2]   Yield 120 mg[5]
Strongly neurotoxic and coagulant[26]. Weakly haemolytic and cytotoxic[26]. Myotoxin is present[14]. The maximum yield has been measured as 400 mg.
Specific antivenom   Taipan[26]
Initial dose of antivenom   12 000 units[26]

Special features   Because of the Taipan's keen senses, they will generally retreat if they have the chance, and consequently they are rarely encountered by humans. In the unfortunate cases where people have been bitten by Taipans, usually the snake has been approached suddenly or was cornered and felt threatened. In these circumstances, Taipans viciously defend themselves, often inflicting multiple bites. Of all the Australian snakes, the Taipan is the most intelligent, nervous, and alert.
Food   Rats are by far the preferred food of Taipans, especially *Melomys* (spp)[38]. However, small birds, mice, bandicoots, and lizards are all recorded as food items.

INLAND TAIPAN *Oxyuranus microlepidotus*

Description Large snake up to 2·5 m, averaging about 2 m. Narrow neck similar to the Taipan but more robust. Head shape is long and rectangular like a Taipan, but slightly shorter with a greater slope from the frontal scale to the rostral. The black eyes of the Inland Taipan are smaller in proportion to those of the Taipan. Fang length is 3·5−6 mm whereas in the Taipan *O. scutellatus* it is 7·9−12·1 mm[38, 40]. (See photographs, pages 63 and 64.)

Scalation Smooth scales. Small dorsal neck scales.

VENTRALS	211−250[41]
SUBCAUDALS	52−70[42] divided
MIDBODIES	23
ANAL	Single

Colour Nearly all specimens have a dark brown to black head. Some have lighter coloured heads. Dorsal coloration pale to dark brown with dark flecks that often form distinct bands posteriorly. Ventral surface yellow. Seasonal colour changes have been recorded[104]. (See photographs, page 63.)

Habits Very little is known about this snake since it occurs in a remote part of Australia and is rarely observed. Its ecology is thought to be closely associated with the occurrence of the Plague Rat, *Rattus villosissimus*, on which it feeds[42]. In contrast to the Taipan *O. scutellatus*, it hangs

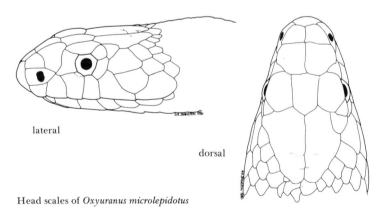

lateral

dorsal

Head scales of *Oxyuranus microlepidotus*

114

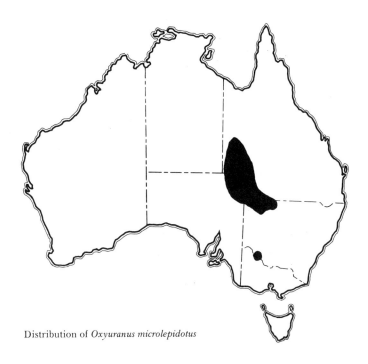

Distribution of *Oxyuranus microlepidotus*

on to its prey when biting. Compared with other venomous snakes it is fairly placid in nature.

Habitat and distribution   Occurs in dry areas of less than 300 mm average annual rainfall and average maximum winter temperatures of about 18°C. Occurs in the Channel country of south-west Queensland and the north-east of South Australia. It has been collected from blacksoil plains and flood plains where it lives in solution holes[106], gibbers, and sand dunes. It appears that areas of greatest population occur on or near the flood plains and channels of the Diamantina River and Cooper Creek. Major vegetation in the area is low saltbush, giant saltbush *Atriplex nummularia*, and lignum bush.

Venom $LD_{50} = 0.01$[2]   Yield   44·2 mg[40]
In 1979 Fohlman pointed out that the venoms of *Oxyuranus scutellatus scutellatus* and *Oxyuranus microlepidotus* were similar and suggested the two were congeneric[43].

115

Inland Taipan was then known as the Small-scaled Snake (*Parademansia microlepidotus*). Both venoms contain direct prothrombin activity and show close similarity in the amino acids of their neurotoxins[43]. The Inland Taipan's venom was found to have a higher level of hyaluronidase activity (spreading factor) than that of the Taipan[40]. The high toxicity and spreading action of the Inland Taipan venom make it the deadliest terrestrial snake known.

Specific antivenom   Taipan[26]
Initial dose of antivenom   12 000 units[26]

Special features   The Inland Taipan has also been known as the Western Taipan, Fierce Snake, Small-scaled Snake, and Lignum Snake. Similarly, the generic history of the snake has been just as unstable. Originally it was referred to as *Diemenia microlepidota* by McCoy in 1879. Since then it has been called one of the Brown Snakes (*Pseudonaja*) and more recently in 1976 it was described by Covacevich *et al.* as *Parademansia microlepidotus*[41]. In 1980 Covacevich *et al.* defined the Taipan and the Inland Taipan as con-generic on the basis of external and cranial morphology, venom, head musculature, hemipenis structure, behaviour, and karyotyping[38].

The original specimens were collected at the junction of the Murray and Darling rivers before 1879. All other known specimens are from the Channel country of the Diamantina River and Cooper Creek area. The collection point of the original specimens is so far from present known habitats that it is now in doubt.

Rediscovery of the snake followed a serious snake bite in 1967 in the Channel country of south-western Queensland. The snake was thought to be a Western Brown Snake, and the patient received Brown Snake antivenom, but responded poorly and suffered a critical illness. The snake was later identified as *Oxyuranus scutellatus*. This greatly extended the range of the Taipan. Covacevich in 1976 described specimens from this area as *Parademansia microlepidotus*, and later in 1980 as *Oxyuranus micro-lepidotus*[38, 41]. Some texts continue to use the Small-scaled Snake as a common name. However, we feel that Inland

Taipan is more appropriate because (1) it is less confusing from a medical standpoint; and (2) small scales occur on both *Oxyuranus scutellatus scutellatus* and *Oxyuranus microlepidotus*.

DEATH ADDERS

There are three species of Death Adders (genus *Acanthophis*) in Australia: the Common Death Adder, Desert Death Adder, and Northern Death Adder. They are very similar in appearance and between the three they occupy nearly all of the Australian mainland.

The Common Death Adder occurs closer to the coast, preferring areas with greater than 250 mm rainfall and slightly cooler areas to those inhabited by the Desert Death Adder. The Northern Death Adder occurs in northern Western Australia and the Northern Territory.

The Desert Death Adder and Northern Death Adder venoms are assumed similar to that of the Common Death Adder.

Habitat destruction or alteration has greatly reduced populations of the Common Death Adder in some areas.

COMMON DEATH ADDER *Acanthophis antarcticus* (Shaw)

Description   Broad triangular head distinct from neck. Short stubby body with a small thin rat-like tail terminat-

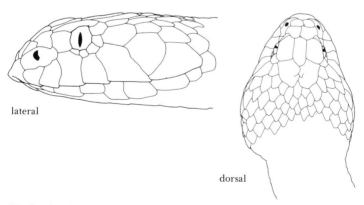

lateral

dorsal

Head scales of *Acanthophis antarcticus*

117

ing in a sharp curved spine. Pupils elliptical. Specimens over 0·915 m have been recorded[17] but average length is about 0·5–0·6 m. (See photographs, pages 65 to 67.)

Scalation Scales on head are almost rugose.

VENTRALS	110–130
SUBCAUDALS	38–55 mostly single
MIDBODIES	21–23 rows
ANAL	Single

Colour General colour highly variable throughout Australia — colour variations exist within localities. Base colour varies from earthy grey to red. Darker transverse bands occur on all Death Adders. Tip of tail is either black or white and is banded in juveniles. Tip of tail usually black in southern Australia and white in northern Australia.

Habits Seeks refuge in leaf litter or loose sand and is nocturnal, being mainly active on hot nights. Captures

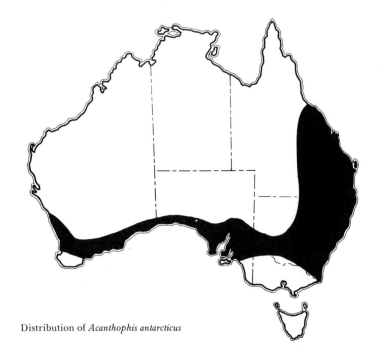

Distribution of *Acanthophis antarcticus*

prey by wriggling grub-like tail as a lure to attract insectivorous creatures. Will not usually retreat if approached by humans. Death Adders are ovoviviparous producing 10–33 young. Shine (1980)[107] concludes that Death Adders only reproduce in alternative years. However, in captivity, one specimen in Whyalla reproduced in three successive years. Other specimens mated at nineteen months gave birth to young at twenty-one months.

Habitat and distribution   Death Adders occur in coastal sand dunes, mallee country, and tropical forests. Virgin habitats appear to be necessary in southern populations and here no evidence exists of long term adaption to drastically modified areas. Their reliance on leaf mulch for refuge and native reptile mammal and bird fauna for food, makes it difficult for Death Adders to tolerate any major changes to their environment.

Venom $LD_{50} = 0.338$[2]   Yield 78 mg[2]
Moderately neurotoxic, weakly haemolytic, and cytolytic. No coagulant activity[26].
Prior to antivenom production, 50% of bites were lethal[1].
Specific antivenom   Death Adder[26]
Initial dose of antivenom   6000 units[26]

Special features   It is possible that sometimes Death Adders lose their tails to their prospective prey, since two specimens found on Eyre Peninsula, South Australia, had only partial tails. This, however, could be a result of incomplete sloughing of skin on the tail causing it to wither and drop off. This has happened to one specimen kept in captivity at Whyalla.

The Death Adder is unique in Australia in both its appearance and habits. Although having a resemblance to a true adder, Death Adders are really elapids, with relatively fixed venom fangs that are not capable of being rotated to the same degree as Viper fangs. Compared with other Australian snakes, Death Adders have long fangs for snakes of their size, averaging about 6 mm[1].

The Death Adder is one group of snakes in Australia that has suffered a dramatic decline in numbers since white man's intervention in Australia. Pressures that have reduced their numbers greatly are habitat change, stocking, and feral animals.

Apart from foxes and cats, in Queensland, introduction of the poisonous cane toad *Bufo marinus* has been a suggested cause for their population reductions. The toads' effects are both direct and indirect. They prey on young Death Adders or kill adult Death Adders after being mouthed or ingested. The reduction in availability of other native animals resulting from the depredations of the cane toad, would also affect the food supply of Death Adders, reducing their population still further.

Food In the wild Death Adders feed on native insectivorous prey such as birds, lizards, and hopping mice. In captivity they thrive on the introduced mouse *Mus musculus* but it is doubtful that they prey on them in the wild since these mice are not insectivorous and are therefore not attracted by the wriggling tail.

DESERT DEATH ADDER *Acanthophis pyrrhus* (Boulenger)

Description Similar in appearance to the Common Death Adder but with a flatter head and the body is more elongate[19]. Grows to 0·75 m[25]. (See photograph, page 68.)

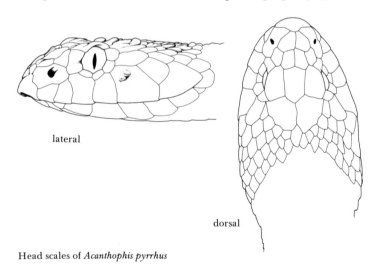

lateral

dorsal

Head scales of *Acanthophis pyrrhus*

Scalation Body scale keeled, head scales rugose and keeled.

VENTRALS	140–160
SUBCAUDALS	45–60 single anterior, divided posterior
MIDBODIES	21
ANAL	Single

Colour The specific name refers to the brick-red colour of the snake and means fire[19]. Dark indistinct cross bands. Ventrally whitish. Tail can be black or white.

Distribution of *Acanthophis pyrrhus*

Habits Assumed to be similar to Common Death Adder. However, little is known about this snake because it occurs in such remote areas.

Habitat and distribution Occurs in dry areas, rocky slopes, and porcupine grass (*Triodia*) areas of inland Australia.

Venom Nothing is known about the venom except that its effect on laboratory animals appears to be rapid.

Specific antivenom   Death Adder[37]

Initial dose of antivenom   6000 units

Special features   The Aborigines have great fear of the snake and call it 'Mythunda'[19]. Its nature is less predictable than that of the Common Death Adder[25].

NORTHERN DEATH ADDER *Acanthophis praelongus* (Ramsay)

Description   Moderately stout, intermediate between the Common Death Adder and Desert Death Adder in rugosty of head shields, keeling of dorsals, and number of ventrals and subcaudals[109]. (See photograph, page 64.)

Scalation

VENTRALS	122–140[108, 109]
SUBCAUDALS	39–57 (19–39 single)[108, 109]
MIDBODIES	Usually 23 (rarely 19, 21)[108, 109]
ANAL	Single[109]

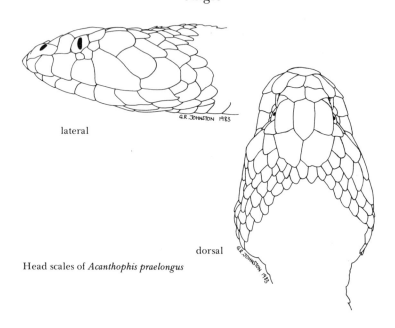

lateral

G.R. JOHNSTON 1983

dorsal

Head scales of *Acanthophis praelongus*

Colour   Darker than the Common Death Adder and Desert Death Adder, stronger colour pattern. Ventral surface, whitish with dark spots[108, 109]

Habits   Assumed to be similar to the Common Death Adder.

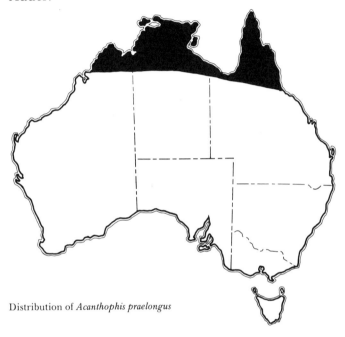

Distribution of *Acanthophis praelongus*

Habitat and distribution   Sub-humid and semi-arid zones of Kimberley Ranges. North of Northern Territory and Queensland and in southern New Guinea[109].

Venom   Unknown
Specific antivenom   Death Adder
Initial dose of antivenom   6000 units

THE BLACK SNAKES

The genus *Pseudechis* has two black-coloured snakes, the Red-bellied Black Snake *P. porphyriacus* and the Spotted Black Snake, *P. guttatus*. The Mulga or King Brown Snake *P. australis* is normally brown to coppery red but does have a black phase in some southern areas. The Colletts Snake *P. colletti* has varied colour patterns on its dorsal surface. *P. butleri* is similar to *P. porphyriacus*, being very dark in colour. The common group name for the genus is therefore somewhat misleading.

Despite marked colour differences, all the *Pseudechis* genus have relatively small frontal scales. This genus occupies nearly all habitat types in Australia with Mulga Snake *Pseudechis australis* being the most widespread and diverse species with possible sub-species differences. The Red-bellied Black Snake *P. porphyriacus* and the Spotted Black Snake *P. guttatus* both occur in areas with rainfall greater than 500 mm per year except in some dry areas along the Murray River where *P. porphyriacus* is resident. This suggests that both of these species are frog-dependent for their food.

RED-BELLIED BLACK SNAKE *Pseudechis porphyriacus* (Shaw)

Description   Average length about 1·25 m[25], maximum length 2·5 m[7]. Head slightly distinct from body. (See photograph, page 68.)

Scalation   Smooth scales.

VENTRALS	180–210
SUBCAUDALS	40–65 first one-third single, remainder divided
MIDBODIES	17
ANAL	Divided

Colour   Fairly uniform in coloration in separate areas throughout its range. Purplish black dorsally with a red to orange ventral surface tending to white in the north. The red is more intense on the outer edges of the belly fading to a lighter colour towards the centre. Underside of tail is black.

Habits   This diurnal snake is usually shy by nature, flattening out its neck when alarmed; it may even attempt mock strikes[7]. Ovoviviparous producing 8–40 young[44].

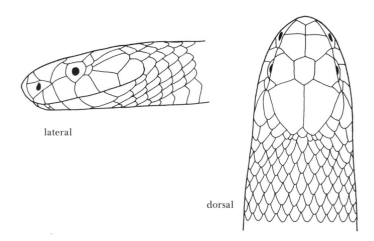

lateral

dorsal

Pseudechis porphyriacus—head scales and distribution

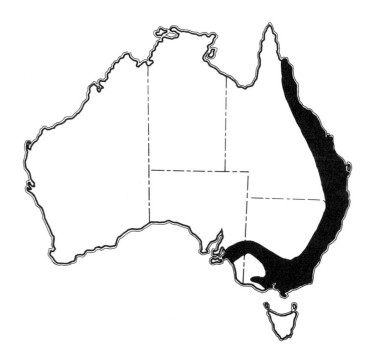

Habitat and distribution Prefers wet areas: swamps, lagoons, streams, and wet forests of eastern Australia and south to south-eastern S.A.

Venom $LD_{50} = 2 \cdot 53$[2] Yield 35 mg[12]
Strong coagulant, haemolytic, and cytotoxic actions. Weakly neurotoxic[26]. Local reactions following a bite are significant in humans but adults are unlikely to die[7]. However, bites are a threat to children[26].
Specific antivenom Tiger Snake or Black Snake[26]
Initial dose of antivenom 3000 units of Tiger or 6000 units of Black Snake[26].

Special features *Food* In the wild the food consists mainly of frogs[18], but small mammals, other snakes, lizards, fish, eels, and birds are taken[7, 25]. The species is recorded to be cannibalistic[25]. It has a distinct body odour.

Very easy to maintain in captivity and a voracious feeder.

MULGA or KING BROWN SNAKE *Pseudechis australis* (Gray)

Description Average maximum length varies from area to area. Maximum length recorded has been in excess of 2·7 m. Average length is about 1·5 m. A robust snake, relatively slow-moving. Very broad head especially with larger specimens. Head slightly distinct from body, sometimes with bulbous cheeks. (See photographs, pages 69 and 70.)

Scalation Large scales.

VENTRALS	189–220
SUBCAUDALS	53–70 all single or all divided or partly single and divided.
MIDBODIES	17
ANAL	Divided

Colour Variable depending on locality. Ranges from light to dark brown, coppery red to nearly yellow. Southern specimens tend to be darker to almost black. Scales are either lighter or darker tipped. Ventral surface usually yellow or yellow-green. Sometimes with orange blotches.

126

Habits   Temperament appears to vary with locality. In southern areas of Eyre Peninsula and west coast of South Australia it is a shy, quiet snake. Northern specimens are reported to be quite excitable when disturbed. They are diurnal in warm weather and become nocturnal in the hotter weather. Worrell records that they are ovoviviparous but Gow has some doubts that this is always the case [7, 25]. Southern specimens (dark coloured) have been observed basking in the winter.

Habitat and distribution   Found over most habitat ranges. Woodlands, mallee, and grass lands, mulga, tropical forests. Rare in Victoria and absent in Tasmania. Does not occur in swamps. Makes its home under large rocks, logs, in rabbit warrens and other animal holes.

Venom $LD_{50} = 1 \cdot 91$[2]   Yield   180 mg[11]
Mulga Snakes are capable of expressing enormous quantities of venom. Up to 600 mg of dried venom has been recorded[7]. The venom's actions are mainly haemolytic and cytoxic but are also mildly neurotoxic and myotoxic[25].
Specific antivenom   Black Snake[26]
Initial dose of antivenom   18 000 units[26]

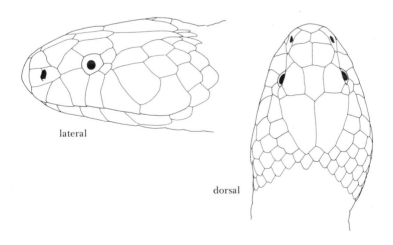

lateral

dorsal

Head scales of *Pseudechis australis*

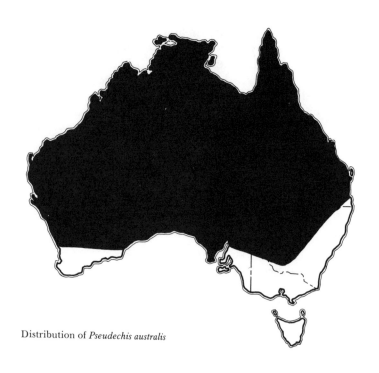

Distribution of *Pseudechis australis*

Special features Mulga Snake venom has a devastating effect on other venomous snakes, but from our experience the venom of other snakes has no apparent effect on Mulga Snakes[45]. When biting, the Mulga Snake has the characteristic of hanging on and chewing into its prey. Mulga Snakes from some areas have unpleasant body odours.

Food Rats, mice, lizards and snakes. In captivity this snake has been found to eat other species of snakes.

COLLETTS or DOWNS TIGER SNAKE *Pseudechis colletti* (Boulenger)

Description Robust body with broad blunt head slightly distinct from body. Average maximum length 2 m. (See photographs, page 71.)

Scalation   Smooth scales

VENTRALS	215–235
SUBCAUDALS	50–70 anterior single, posterior divided
MIDBODIES	19
ANAL	Divided

Colour   Is probably the most colourful of our venomous snakes. Light brown, dark brown to black with salmon to red scales forming irregular bands. Cream to orange ventrally.

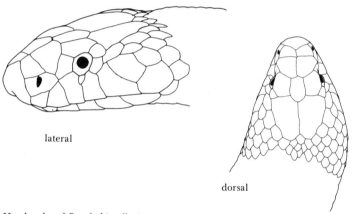

lateral

dorsal

Head scales of *Pseudechis colletti*

Habits   Very little is known about this snake, probably because it occurs in a remote area. Like other members of this genus, it has an offensive body odour when handled. Oviparous producing 12 or more young[7].

Habitat and distribution   Central Queensland, non-swampy drier inland areas[25].

Venom $LD_{50} = 2·36$ (saline)[2]   Yield   30 mg[10]. This is only approximately comparable to other figures quoted throughout the book.
Specific antivenom   Black Snake
Initial dose of antivenom   18 000 units

129

Distribution of *Pseudechis colletti*

Special features   Known to be cannibalistic[25]. Feeds on lizards and small mammals.

SPOTTED BLACK SNAKE *Pseudechis guttatus* (De Vis)

Description   Head indistinct from body. Grows to 2 m. Fang length about 3·5 mm[15]. (See photographs, page 72.)

Scalation   Smooth scales.
VENTRALS	175–205
SUBCAUDALS	45–65 anterior single, posterior divided
MIDBODIES	19
ANAL	Divided

Colour   Dorsally it may be glossy black, sometimes with a few cream coloured scales. Some specimens are cream with black tipped scales. Ventral surface blue grey.

130

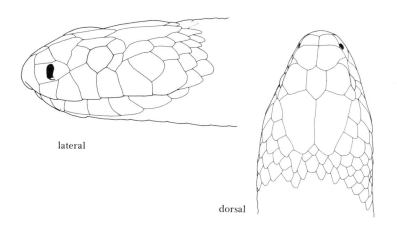

lateral

dorsal

Pseudechis guttatus — head scales and distribution

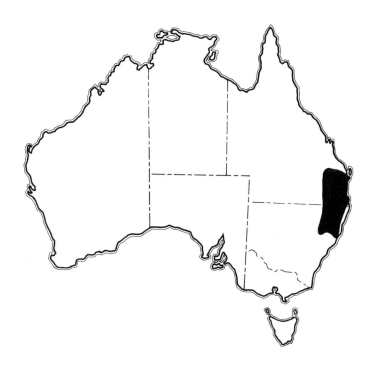

Habits Oviparous producing up to 16 eggs[25]. Flattens out its whole body when annoyed[7].

Habitat and distribution Drier areas of north-eastern New South Wales and south-eastern Queensland extending inland.

Venom $LD_{50} = 1 \cdot 53$[2]
The venom contains coagulants, haemolysins, neurotoxins, and cytotoxins[15].
Specific antivenom Black Snake or Tiger Snake[26]
Initial dose of antivenom 6000 units Black Snake or 3000 units Tiger Snake[26].

BUTLERS SNAKE *Pseudechis butleri* (Smith)

Description A large snake growing to a maximum of 1·6 m in length. Head moderately distinct from body[110]. (See photograph, page 70.)

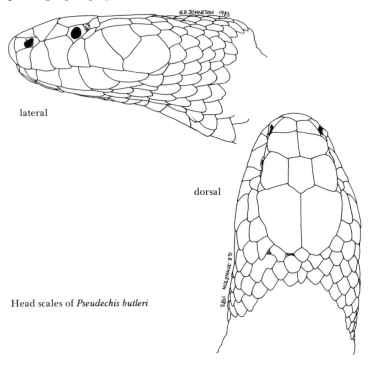

lateral

dorsal

Head scales of *Pseudechis butleri*

132

Scalation

VENTRALS	204–216[110]
SUBCAUDALS	55–65 (35–76% undivided)[110]
MIDBODIES	17[110]
ANAL	Divided[110]

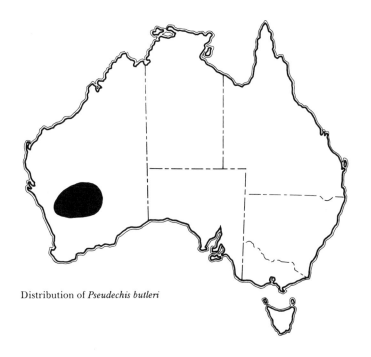

Distribution of *Pseudechis butleri*

Colour　Reddish-brown on the rostral, nasals, preoculars, labials (except for a short black sub-ocular streak bordering orbit), chin shields, and gulars. Black on the remainder of head and nape with reddish-brown tinge. Reddish-brown on head and neck more prominent in juveniles. Remainder of dorsal scales black with yellow centres. Ventral surface bright yellow with black flecks and an uneven black edge at base[110].

Habits　Unknown

Habitat and distribution　Arid mid-west of Western Australia[110].

Venom   Nothing is known about the venom.
Specific antivenom   Tiger Snake or Black Snake
Initial dose of antivenom   3000 units of Tiger or 18 000 units of Black Snake.

THE COPPERHEADS

Storr (1982)[102] includes Copperheads *Austrelaps* in his concept of *Notechis*. Rawlinson suggests there could be three separate forms. They are:

1. Highland form
2. Lowland form
3. Pygmy form (Adelaide Hills and Kangaroo Island)

The lowland and highland forms occur in areas of greater than 450 mm rainfall annually with summer maximum temperatures ranging from 18°C–21°C in Tasmania and Bass Strait Islands, to 24°C–33°C on the mainland of Australia.

The pygmy species occurs in areas with 600–800 mm rainfall per year and a mild summer maximum of 23°C–25°C average.

COPPERHEAD *Austrelaps superbus* (Gunther)

Description   Head small and slightly distinct from body. Attains 1·7 m, but averages about 0·9 m. Pygmy Copperheads are much smaller. Eye large, round pupil. (See photographs, pages 73 and 74.)

Scalation   Smooth scales

VENTRALS	140–165
SUBCAUDALS	35–55 single
MIDBODIES	15 (rarely 13 or 17)
ANAL	Single

Colour   Dorsal colour variations are: black, brown, tan, coppery, and light grey. Some specimens possess a dark vertebral stripe and dark band across the nape. Belly is cream to grey. The labial scales are often strikingly barred.

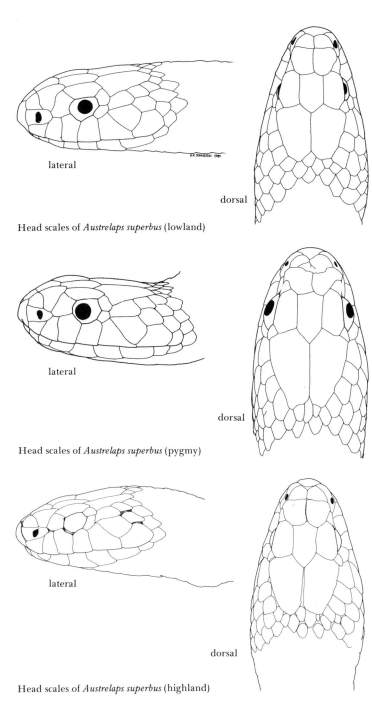

lateral

dorsal

Head scales of *Austrelaps superbus* (lowland)

lateral

dorsal

Head scales of *Austrelaps superbus* (pygmy)

lateral

dorsal

Head scales of *Austrelaps superbus* (highland)

135

Habits One of the best distinguishing features of the Copperhead is its low temperature tolerance (or preference). Copperheads are active earlier in spring and later in autumn than other snakes. Nocturnal in warm weather. Usually inoffensive, quick to retreat. Occur in large colonies. Ovoviviparous; up to 20 young have been recorded.

Habitat and distribution Occurs in the south-eastern highlands and surrounding swamplands. Has been recorded from mainland Tasmania, Kangaroo Island, Adelaide Hills, Flinders Island, King Island, Hunter Island, Preservation Island, and Great Dog Island[34, 46].

Venom $LD_{50} = 0.50$[2] Yield 24.9 mg[13]
The venom is strongly neurotoxic, haemolytic, and cytotoxic[26].
Specific antivenom Tiger Snake[26]
Initial dose of antivenom 3000 units[26]

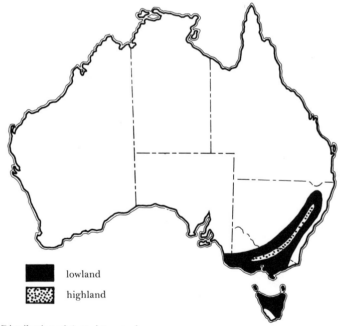

lowland

highland

Distribution of *Austrelaps superbus*

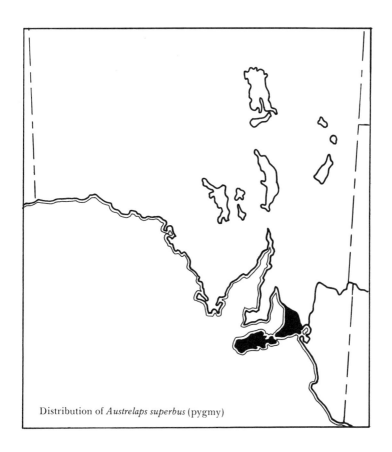

Distribution of *Austrelaps superbus* (pygmy)

Special features   *Food*   The main diet comprises either frogs or tadpoles. On occasions they will eat snakes, mice, and lizards.

THE BROAD-HEADED SNAKES

The Broad-headed snakes (genus *Hoplocephalus*) all occur along the eastern coast and are characterised by their broad heads, keeled ventral scales, and smooth dorsal scales.

Throughout their range the average rainfall exceeds 800 mm and the summer average maximum is about 30°C.

137

PALE-HEADED SNAKE *Hoplocephalus bitorquatus* (Jan)

Description   Broad flat head distinct from body. Varies in length from 0·5–0·9 m. (See photograph, page 75.)

Scalation   Smooth scales.
VENTRALS	190–225 keeled
SUBCAUDALS	40–65 single
MIDBODIES	19 or 21
ANAL	Single

Colour   The dorsal colour is light brown to grey with a white or cream band on the nape. There is lighter grey colouring on the head interspersed with dark grey scales. The ventral surface is creamy grey, occasionally with darker flecks.

Habits   Mostly arboreal and lives under free bark where it feeds on geckoes and lizards. Easily aroused assuming a threat posture at the slightest disturbance. Ovoviviparous.

Habitat and distribution   Rain forest, wet sclerophyll forest to dry sclerophyll forest and woodlands.

Venom   Yield   1·66 mg[9]   (Single milking record.) Very little known at this stage.

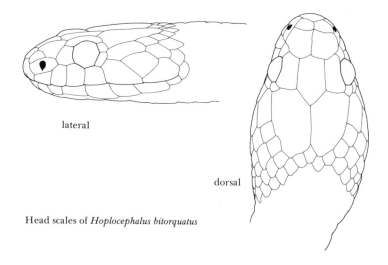

lateral

dorsal

Head scales of *Hoplocephalus bitorquatus*

138

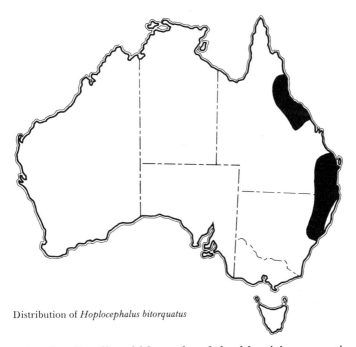

Distribution of *Hoplocephalus bitorquatus*

Joe Bredl suffered blurred and double vision, sweating, breathing difficulty, and headache within 10 minutes of a bite from a specimen 0·76 m long[47].

Specific antivenom　Tiger Snake*
Initial dose of antivenom　3000 units*
*Assumed the same as for *H. bungaroides*[26]

STEPHENS BANDED SNAKE *Hoplocephalus stephensi* (Krefft)

Description　Broad flat head, distinct from body. Varies from 0·5 m to 1 m in length. (See photograph, page 75.)

Scalation　Smooth scales.

VENTRALS	220–250 keeled
SUBCAUDALS	50–70 single
MIDBODIES	21
ANAL	Single

Colour　Dorsally black with narrow cream crossbands. Unbanded specimens occur on occasions. On the ventral

139

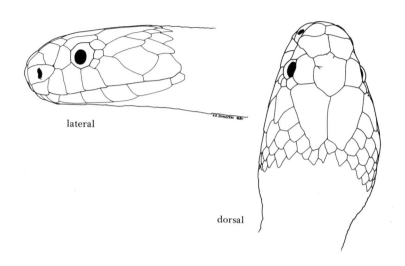

lateral

dorsal

Hoplocephalus stephensi—head scales and distribution

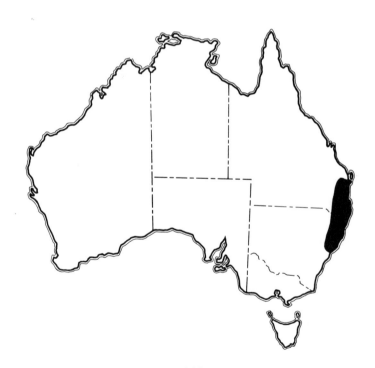

surface they are cream with black spots tending to uniform black at the tip of tail.

Habits Ill-tempered snake, usually difficult to keep in captivity. An arboreal snake that takes refuge behind loose bark or in tree hollows. Nocturnal.

Habitat and distribution Wet sclerophyll or rainforests of the east coast.

Venom $LD_{50} = 1 \cdot 44^2$
Specific antivenom Tiger Snake*
Initial dose of antivenom 3000 units*
*Assumed the same as for *H. bungaroides*[26]

Special features Gow records that it is ovoviviparous—5 young have been observed[25]. The main threat to its survival lies in the future of the rainforests in its range.
Food Feeds on geckoes and skinks; sometimes large specimens in captivity accept mice.

BROAD-HEADED SNAKE *Hoplocephalus bungaroides* (Schlegel)

Description Head distinct from body. Broad head. (See photographs, page 76.)

Scalation Smooth scales.
VENTRALS	200–230 keeled
SUBCAUDALS	40–65 single
MIDBODIES	21
ANAL	Single

Colour Jet black dorsally with narrow yellow cross bands. Labial scales barred with black and yellow. Head black with yellow spots.

Habits Feeds on lizards and frogs. Nocturnal. Herpetologists find this one of the more difficult snakes to handle.

Habitat and description Lives in a restricted area of about 250 km radius of Sydney, mainly living under sandstone rocks. Its main population occurs in the Hawkesbury sand-

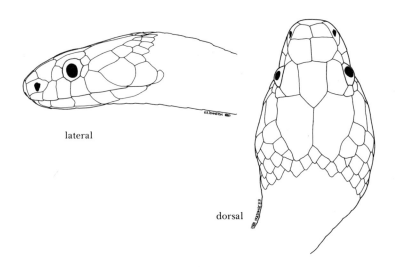

lateral

dorsal

Hoplocephalus bungaroides — head scales and distribution

142

stone formation[25, 44]. Worrell records that it also lives in hollow trees during summer[7].

Venom   Gow has reported that the venom is neurotoxic[25]. Worrell reported that envenomation caused a violent headache, vomiting, partial blindness, perspiration, and muscular weakness[7].

Specific antivenom   Tiger Snake[26]
Initial dose of antivenom   3000 units[26]

Special features   Ovoviviparous giving birth to 8–20 young[7, 44]. Because of restricted range, much of which is situated in a highly populated area, it is the opinion of the authors that this snake is an endangered species and its legal protection is fully supported.

MISCELLANEOUS SNAKES

ROUGH-SCALED SNAKE *Tropidechis carinatus* (Krefft)

Description   Broad head, distinct from body. Grows to almost 1 m but averages about 0·7 m. Large eye. Superficially resembles the harmless fresh water snake *Amphiesma mairii* and is sympatric with it in part of its range. Possesses large fangs[7, 25, 44]. (See photograph, page 76.)

Scalation   Dorsal scales strongly keeled.
VENTRALS	160–185
SUBCAUDALS	50–60 single
MIDBODIES	23
ANAL	Single

Colour   Dorsally it is olive green to dark brown with dark blotches forming cross bands. Ventral surface is creamish with darker blotches.

Habits   Feeds mainly on frogs but also takes lizards and mice in captivity. Very alert and nervous. Herpetologists find it very difficult to handle safely. Both diurnal and nocturnal.

Habitat and description   Prefers areas near water. Found in wet sclerophyll forests or rainforests. Most common in the Clarence River district of New South Wales.

143

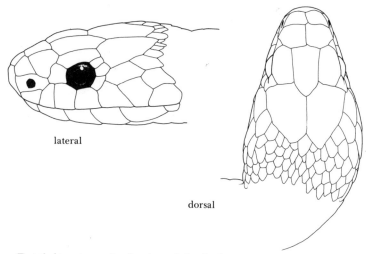

lateral

dorsal

Tropidechis carinatus — head scales and distribution

Venom $LD_{50} = 1.09$[2]   Yield 6 mg[11]
Strongly coagulant, moderately neurotoxic, haemolytic, and cytotoxic[26]. Lethal bites have occurred.
Specific antivenom   Tiger Snake[26]
Initial dose of antivenom   3000 units [26]

Special features   Often referred to as the Clarence River snake. Will defend itself vigorously if molested or threatened. Very nervous snake when kept in captivity. A specimen kept at Whyalla for over 3 years is as nervous now as it was when caught, and has been almost impossible to handle.

SMALL-EYED SNAKE *Cryptophis nigrescens* (Gunther)

Description   Grows to 1.2 m. Head distinct from body. (See photograph, page 76.)

Colour   Shiny blue-black dorsally. Ventrally white, cream, or pink, sometimes with darker blotches.

Scalation   Smooth scales
VENTRALS	165–210
SUBCAUDALS	30–46 single
MIDBODIES	15
ANAL	Single

Habits   Nocturnal. Feeds mainly on geckoes and small skinks, occasionally frogs[25]. Ovoviviparous, producing up to 5 young. The young measure 10–12 cm[25].

Habitat and description   Sandstone areas, well timbered country, rocky areas. Found under rocks, in crevices, earth cracks, or under the bark of fallen trees. They have been found hibernating together in large numbers[25].

Venom $LD_{50} = 2.67$ (saline)[2]   Yield 8 mg[14]
The average lethal dose is only roughly comparable to other figures in this book. Pollitt studied electrophoretic patterns of the venom and found that it was easy to distinguish from other Australian snake venoms. Experimental work has shown that the venom is rich in myotoxic activity (i.e. muscle necrosis). The myotoxic function is

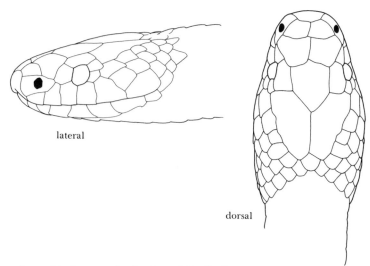

lateral

dorsal

Cryptophis nigrescens—head scales and distribution

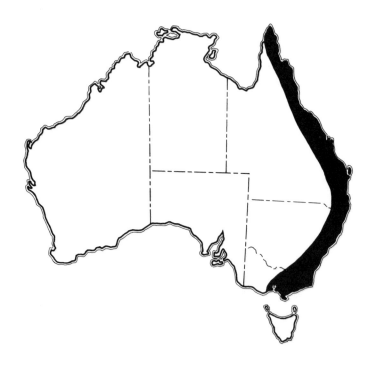

146

called cryptoxin. Destruction of muscle continues for days after envenomation. Death may result due to dehydration, renal failure, and inhalational pneumonia[14].

Specific antivenom   Tiger Snake*
Initial dose of antivenom   3000 units*
*This is suggested as a first step. Contact Commonwealth Serum Laboratories if complications occur.

BLACK WHIP SNAKE *Demansia atra* (Macleay)

Description   Average length 1 m. Head narrow; whip-like body. (See photograph, page 77.)

Colour   Dorsally light to dark olive brown to black. Each dorsal scale is rimmed with a darker colour and greenish sides. Dark pigment more pronounced towards the tail. Top of head usually has dark spots or flecks. Ventrally yellowy green and reddish towards tail tip[44].

Scalation   Smooth scales.

VENTRALS	160–220
SUBCAUDALS	70–105 divided
MIDBODIES	15
ANAL	Divided

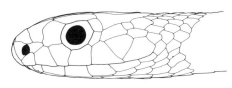

lateral

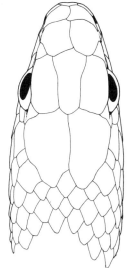

dorsal

Head scales of *Demansia atra*

147

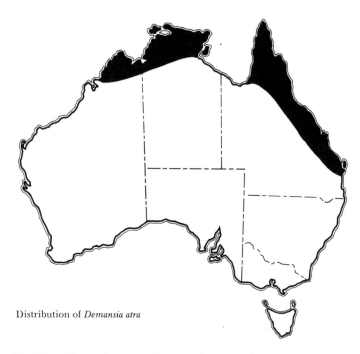

Distribution of *Demansia atra*

Habits Very fast-moving snake. Produces 8–20 eggs[7, 25]. Feeds mainly on lizards and possibly frogs and small mammals[25].

Habitat and distribution Found in the drier areas of woodland habitat.

Venom LD_{50} greater than 14·2 (saline)[2]. This is only roughly comparable with other lethal doses in this book.

Gow reported a bite on the hand that produced severe local pain and also swelling of the hand and arm that took one week to subside[25]. Worrell recorded a bite that caused him local pain and swelling that subsided. It recurred three times in a fortnight accompanied by tiny pustular pimples[7].

Specific antivenom   Tiger Snake*

Initial dose of antivenom   3000 units*

*This is suggested as a first step. Contact Commonwealth Serum Laboratories if complications arise.

Chapter 5
CONSERVATION

In 1976 the House of Representatives Standing Committee on Environment and Conservation[48] made its second report to the Parliament of the Commonwealth of Australia. Included in the report was the recommendation that the Federal Government give additional financial support to the Biological Resources Survey (and to other surveys being conducted), to establish firmly the extent of Australia's wildlife populations. Of the many other recommendations of the Standing Committee's Report, this one is probably the most important. Even with additional funding, to determine the complete distribution information and population density levels of Australia's wildlife populations will require the combined efforts of scientific bodies, para-professionals, and other interested people.

In the same report, the Committee concluded that 'little information is available on the population and distribution of Australian reptiles and an assessment of the species which may be threatened by commercial exploitation is not possible.' Dangerous venomous snakes described in this book fall into this category.

Although there is a paucity of such information on the snakes covered in this book, all Australian States have passed legislation introducing legal protection in one form or another. In attempting to obtain an overall picture of the protection afforded these snakes, and their true status, the authors contacted National Parks and Wildlife departments in each State and asked them to advise on the legal protection and the department's assessment of the population status in their respective State. To try and standardise the information, they were asked to conform with the ICUN (International Union for Conservation of Nature and National Resources) Red Data Book terminology of endangered, vulnerable, and rare[49]. The terminology can be defined thus:

Common Name	Scientific name	Vic.	S.A.	W.A.	N.T.	Tas.	N.S.W.	Qld	Comment
Common Tiger Snake	Notechis scutatus	P / S	P / unknown				P / S	P / S	
Peninsula Tiger Snake	N. ater niger		P / unknown						
Kreffts Tiger Snake	N. ater ater		P / unknown						
Western Tiger Snake	N. ater occidentalis			N / S					
Chappell Island Tiger Snake	N. ater serventyi					N / S			
Tasmanian and King Island Tiger Snake	N. ater humphreysi					N / S			
Common Death Adder	Acanthophis antarcticus	P / unknown*	P / unknown	N / S	P / S		P / S	P / S	*Mainly in other States
Desert Death Adder	A. pyrrhus		P / unknown	N / S	P / S		P / S	P / unknown	
Common Brown Snake	Pseudonaja textilis textilis	P / S	P / unknown		P / rare and uncertain		P / S	P / S	
Western Brown Snake	P. nuchalis	P / R*	P / unknown	N / S	P / S		P / S	P / S	*Mainly in other States
Dugite	P. affinis affinis		P / unknown	N / S					
Peninsula Brown Snake	P. affinis inframacula		P / unknown						
Tanners Brown Snake	P. affinis tanneri			N / R*					*See ref. 50
Ingrams Brown Snake	P. ingrami				P / S			P / unknown	
Speckled Brown Snake	P. guttata				P / S			P / unknown	
Red-bellied Black Snake	Pseudechis porphyriacus	P / unknown	P / unknown				P / S	P / S	
Mulga Snake	P. australis	P / unknown	P / unknown	N / S	P / S		P / S	P / S	
	P. colletti							P / S	

Common Name	Scientific Name						Notes
Spotted Black Snake	*P. guttatus*				P / S	P / S	
Taipan	*Oxyuranus scutellatus scutellatus*	P / status unknown	P / uncertain		P / S	P / S	Only 1 spec. from W.A.
Inland Taipan	*Oxyuranus microlepidotus*	P / 2 collected 1879•	P / unknown		P / R•	P / S	•Thinly distributed information lacking
Copperhead	*Austrelaps superbus*						
lowland		P / S	P / unknown	N / S	P / S		
highland		P / S			P / S		
pygmy			P / unknown				
Rough-scaled Snake	*Tropidechis carinatus*				P / V•	P / S	•Thinly distributed in habitat
Black Whip Snake	*Demansia atra*	N / S				P / S	
Small-eyed Snake	*Cryptophis nigrescens*	P / S				P / S	
Stephens Banded Snake	*Hoplocephalus stephensi*				P / V•	P / S	•Habitat dest. may further limit species
Broad-headed Snake	*H. bungaroides*				P / R•		•Distribution scattered over restricted area. Most areas now in reserves
Pale-headed Snake	*H. bitorquatus*				P / S	P / S	

Table 5.1 *State Governments' assessment of dangerous terrestrial snakes*[51]

Endangered (E)   Snakes in danger of extinction and whose survival is unlikely if the causal endangering factors continue to operate. They may be snakes whose numbers have been reduced to a critical level or whose habitats are confined to a small area or which have been destroyed to such an extent that snakes existing in them may be considered to be in immediate danger of extinction.

Vulnerable (V)   Snakes believed likely to become endangered if the causal factors continue operating. These factors can be, for instance, over-exploitation of the environment or extensive habitat destruction.

Rare (R)   Snakes that are not at present endangered or vulnerable but are at risk. They are usually snakes that are either localised within restricted geographical areas or habitats, or thinly scattered over an extensive range.

Threatened (T)   This is a collective term to describe the above three terms.

In this book the term *Safe* (S) is used to describe snakes that are not threatened in any way.

Other symbols used are:

P   = Protected
N   = Not protected
—   = Not known to occur in that State

The results of the inter-State survey are summarised in Table 5.1.

It should be noted that although Western Australia lists some species as unprotected, permits are still required to collect those specimens from the wild.

Using State departmental information combined with the authors' expertise and other herpetological opinions a further Table can be drawn up presenting a summarised national picture of the status of each species.

Habitat destruction is one of the main contributors to the population decrease of any species. (See photograph, page 77.) Habitat modification also causes the decline of most species. Exceptions to this rule are probably some of the Brown Snakes (genus *Pseudonaja*) that seem to benefit from changes to their habitat, mainly involving grain production. These areas, however, usually retain little pockets such as rock piles, rubbish dumps, piles of cleared scrub, clumps of uncleared land, stone walls, or introduced vegetation that support abundant populations of lizards, essential food for the survival of juvenile Brown Snakes. The adult Brown Snakes thrive on introduced mice *Mus musculus*, and indeed usually grow larger when feeding on these animals.

Peter Mirtschin has been involved in a pilot study to try and remove the South African Boxthorn bush from the Sir Joseph Banks Archipelago in Spencer Gulf, South Australia. These bushes are rapidly increasing in number and are displacing the native vegetation. Winceby Island is a small island in the group and the worst affected by Boxthorns, and it appears that the Tiger Snake population has been drastically reduced on that island and may even be extinct. It is not known to what extent South African Boxthorn bushes have influenced the snakes. However, the bushes could only have long-term detrimental effects. (See photograph, page 78.)

Although there are exceptions to population decline due to habitat change, most species are adversely affected. Death Adders are probably among the best examples of a snake affected by habitat change. Because they rely on leaf litter for refuge and on the maintenance at natural levels of native lizards, mammals, and birdlife for food, disruptions to these requirements usually result in the rapid decline of the Death Adder population. Copperheads and Tiger Snakes also suffer from habitat change involving the removal of swamps or stone walls that provide their food and refuge[8].

In the Riverland district along the Murray River in South Australia, Tiger Snakes were once abundant, but over the last ten years their numbers have been seriously diminished. While many have been killed by humans, there are significantly large areas where humans rarely go, that also are now deficient in Tiger Snake population. It is hard to determine the major cause of this population reduction, but one explanation is that irrigation and

Common name	Scientific name	Status	Comments
Common Tiger Snake	*Notechis scutatus*	S	Habitat reduced but still safe
Peninsula Tiger Snake	*N. ater niger*	S	
Kreffts Tiger Snake	*N. ater ater*	R	Very small range Nat. Parks/pastoral
Chappell Island Tiger Snake	*N. ater serventyi*	S	
Tasmanian and King Island Tiger Snake	*N. ater humphreysi*	S	
Western Tiger Snake	*N. ater occidentalis*	S	
Common Death Adder	*Acanthophis antarcticus*	S	Greatly reduced in population but still common in virgin country
Desert Death Adder	*A. pyrrhus*	S	
Common Brown Snake	*Pseudonaja textilis textilis*	S	Rare in N.T.
Peninsula Brown Snake	*P. textilis inframacula*	S	
Western Brown Snake	*P. nuchalis*	S	
Dugite	*P. affinis affinis*	S	
Tanners Brown Snake	*P. affinis tanneri*	R	Only occurs in Recherche Archipelago and Rottnest Island
Speckled Brown Snake	*P. guttata*	S	
Ingrams Brown Snake	*P. ingrami*	S	
Red-bellied Black Snake	*Pseudechis porphyriacus*	S	
Mulga Snake	*P. australis*	S	
Colletts Snake	*P. colletti*	S	
Spotted Black Snake	*P. guttatus*	S	
Rough-scaled Snake	*Tropidechis carinatus*	S	V. N.S.W. Thinly distributed over area subjected to habitat destruction
Taipan	*Oxyuranus scutellatus*	S	
Inland Taipan	*Oxyuranus microlepidotus*	S	R. N.S.W. Thinly distributed, information lacking
Copperhead	*Austrelaps superbus*		
	lowland	S	
	highland	S	
	pygmy	V	Small range, threat of urbanisation taking habitat. Rare on K.I.

Table 5.2

Black Whip Snake	*Demansia atra*	S	
Small-eyed Snake	*Cryptophis nigrescens*	S	
Stephens Banded Snake	*Hoplocephalus stephensi*	S	V. N.S.W. Habitat destruction may further limit species
Broad-headed Snake	*H. bungaroides*	E	Small range in close proximity to urban Sydney
Pale-headed Snake	*H. bitorquatus*	S	

Table 5.2   *Overall conservation status of dangerous terrestrial snakes*

water consumption, coupled with the water-level control system of locks, has increased the salinity in the area, reducing frog populations and thus decreasing the major component of this snake's diet.

Man has introduced many exotic animals into Australia, each of which affects our native animals in one way or another. While some may have been beneficial for snakes, others have been disastrous. Probably the exotic animal most concerned with native reptile destruction is the feral cat. It has been shown in one survey carried out by the Sturt College of Advanced Education (Adelaide) that reptiles comprise about 32 per cent of the diet of cats in arid areas[52]. Since cats are fairly resistant to snake venom[53, 54], they pose a considerable threat to native snake fauna. Juvenile snakes are more prone to attack by cats since they are slower, less able to protect themselves, and occur in greater numbers.

The cane toad *Bufo marinus* is thought to have affected snakes in Queensland. It was introduced into north-east Queensland in 1935 from Hawaii as a biological control measure for the Grey-back Beetle, a pest to the sugar industry[55]. By 1941 it was found that the cane toad was having little effect on the Grey-back beetle but was becoming a pest to both the native fauna and human residents of the area. Today the cane toad's range stretches from Cape York to northern New South Wales and across westwards into the Northern Territory, and is proving to be a threat to many of our native animals. There is only one native animal, the Keelback snake *Amphiesma mairii*, that is known to prey on the cane toad successfully. Despite recorded predation on the toad by other animals, there is definite evidence of deaths in snakes caused by ingesting the poisonous cane toad. There are recorded deaths of Black Snakes, Brown Snakes, Death Adders, and Tiger Snakes[55] attributed to the cane toad, and no doubt most, if not all, large elapids occurring in the range of the cane toad would be affected in a similar way.

Other feral animals such as goats, horses, donkeys, pigs, and camels all have an effect on the environment. The net result of their introduction and effects on the venomous snakes is a little more subtle than that of the cane toad or feral cat. Nevertheless, their impact may well be worse. They are all large grazing animals depriving some of our smaller native mammals and birds of food; some insects, too, have less food, and the decline in insect population affects skinks and dragons. The overall result is that there is less potential snake food.

Fire and floods are both natural phenomena and wildlife has evolved to cope with these hazards, provided that near the burnt and flooded areas there are sufficient areas to support some of the surviving wildlife until regeneration occurs. White man's presence has increased the chance of fire by a factor of from 7 to 20 times[56], and for snakes, fires at the wrong time of the year in fragile areas are detrimental.

Deliberate burning off for grazing or cropping in the Northern Territory and Queensland must have a drastic effect on the reptile wildlife. Repetition of these fires in the same areas, rather than natural randomness, soon wipes out many species.

Floods along the Murray and Lachlan rivers during the winter have been responsible for many Tiger Snake deaths. Worrell records that on the Lachlan River in 1952 the icy water killed hundreds of Tiger Snakes[34] which had stiffened and drowned. Unnatural flooding by use of the locks has also had a similar effect[57].

156

The flood plain of the Diamantina River normally supports a population of many snakes and a profitable cattle industry. In 1974 the river flooded and in places was 70 kilometres wide. Before the flood, station owners reported an abundance of snakes, but since then, where the flood plain has dried out, snakes have not returned in the same numbers[58]. As with the cattle many would have been washed away with the flood. This area is the home of the Inland Taipan (*Oxyuranus microlepidotus*) and recent expeditions to the area have confirmed their presence throughout the range; but not in the numbers that were once present.

Snake populations should be able to withstand the pressures of natural disasters. If, however, natural forces are coupled with some unnatural force such as overgrazing or introduced predators, the effects are more severe[59].

All States have enacted legislation to protect most native animals, including dangerously venomous snakes, and this on the surface appears to be in keeping with the principles of good conservation; but there are some drawbacks. From the reports of the House of Representatives' Standing Committee 1976, it was concluded that biological surveys were one of the most urgent requirements in the protection of Australia's wildlife. To obtain a picture of the distribution of any animal and its population density, sample specimens must be collected both from new and from established areas. As well as providing data allowing conservationists to establish range and density, specimen collection is also required for other scientific studies. The new protective legislation has made it very difficult and frustrating for ecologists and scientists wishing to conduct surveys and to mount research programmes.

There are three main problems facing scientists, ecologists, para-professionals, and other people working in this field.

1. Each State has its own specific legislation and way of managing this legislation. Studying animals that occur in other States presents the problem of collection and removal

157

from that State. Inevitably there are delays in permit issue and often export permits granted in one State expire by the time import permits are granted in the other State.

2.   The knowledge of wildlife officers in most States is deficient in reptiles. This causes problems when officers are deciding whether to grant permits, because they tend to err on the safe side and refuse. This is extremely frustrating for people specialising in certain areas.

3.   Most State wildlife departments are unfortunately under the misconception that collecting animals from the wild is a major threat to population numbers. There is, however, widespread opinion that this activity affects only populations that are threatened. The protection laws place great emphasis on law enforcement, which has very dubious general value for conservation. Law enforcement has an important role to play where threatened species are involved but has questionable value where animals are categorised as 'safe'. Those in favour of law enforcement argue that they are unable to discriminate between those species requiring protection and those that do not. This type of blanket legislation is akin to 'putting every single Australian person in prison, on the quite legitimate argument that police are unable to distinguish innocent citizens from the few criminals in their midst.' (M. Tyler, 'On Australian Amphibians'[49].)

To overcome these problems, conservation in Australia requires a uniform approach. It requires the weight of the Federal Government behind it. This would rationalise current State departments, pool resources, and abolish the necessity for the current import/export system for moving animals from one State to another within Australia.

Under a uniform system all snakes (and all animals in the like category) that are 'safe' should be made available by permit for any reasonable purpose.

Of the snakes covered in this book, the snakes in Table

5.3 are classified as threatened and require stringent protection.

Name	Scientific name	Reason
Kreffts Tiger Snake	*Notechis ater ater*	Small range some of which is covered in National Parks
Broad-headed Snake	*Hoplocephalus bungaroides*	Small range most of which is urbanised
Stephens Banded Snake	*Hoplocephalus stephensi*	V. N.S.W. only due to habitat destruction
Copperhead	*Austrelaps superbus* (pygmy race)	Some of habitat in National Parks but much being urbanised. Rare on Kangaroo Island
Tanners Brown Snake	*Pseudonaja affinis tanneri*	Rare—only occurs on Box Island, Recherche Archipelago, and Rottnest Island
Rough-scaled Snake	*Tropidechis carinatus*	V. N.S.W. only. Limited knowledge. Safe in Qld.

Table 5.3   *Threatened dangerous terrestrial snakes*

Zoos and reptile parks also have a role to play in conservation. One of the main themes of conservation today is conveying the message to the people. This is being done by using various television programmes, books, newspapers, and by presenting talks to interested groups. Another method, involving removal from the wild, is exhibiting live animals in museums, zoos, and reptile parks.

In the past little attempt was made to understand captive breeding, but with increasing legislative pressure on collecting from the wild, reptile parks and zoos have been forced to take a greater interest in this field. Although captive breeding does not really significantly reduce the drain on wild populations, it has helped in the understanding of some snakes. This knowledge will help future rehabilitation programmes. Provided the causal factors that resulted in the decline of a particular snake are removed or minimised, populations artificially bolstered from captive-bred stock could be established.

Peter Mirtschin has been actively studying the breeding of the Common Death Adder for about six years and has had reasonable success in breeding them. One of the problems with Death Adders is that the juveniles are quite small when born and their natural food is small skinks. The problem of collecting many small skinks is prohibitive in trying to raise a large number of Death Adders. A successful technique that will raise the young to adulthood with a 90–100 per cent success rate has been developed. The method used is to make up a battery of cages (see photograph, page 78), provide a small section of the floor with a heating pad, and keep each little Adder separate. So successful is this technique that even a grotesquely deformed Adder has been raised to adulthood. (See photograph, page 78.) Offered as food are small day-old mice, graduating to larger mice as the Adders get bigger. Normally the very young Adders show no interest in the mice but if the head of the day-old mouse is placed in the snake's mouth it will eventually bite on the mouse and start eating. This procedure is carried out for about five to six months, after which most of them will take mice on their own.

Growth rate for small Death Adders is rapid and in the first twelve months will follow a parabolic relationship of about $W = 1 \cdot 2T^2$ (where W = weight of Death Adder in grams and T = time in months). Such information may be useful in rehabilitation exercises when areas are being surveyed as to their suitability for the release of captive-bred animals.

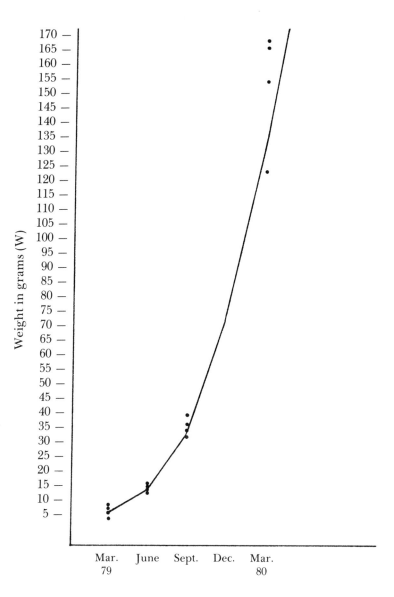

Table 5.4

	March	June	September	March
A	5·02	12·11	34·29	165
B	5·32	14·54	29·61	122
C	4·39	12·55	38·66	168
D	5·18	11·16	31·32	152

$W = 1·2T^2$
where 1·2 is constant for first 12 months
feeding at maximum.
A, B, C, and D are different Death Adders.

Table 5.4   *Increase in Death Adder weight (gm) with time*

Venomous snakes kept in captivity are always useful for scientific venom research. Periodically requests for venom are received from the Commonwealth Serum Laboratories and venom has been sent as far away as Japan for study. Milking venom from snakes is a relatively harmless operation for the snake if done correctly. There are a few traumatic moments for the snake while it is held and forced to bite over a rubber diaphragm.

Snake venoms, being complex mixtures of organic proteins and enzymes, are being studied by various people around the world in the hope that one or more of their components may eventually prove useful in the field of medicine. This has happened already, of course, but no doubt much more remains to be discovered from the study of venoms. As pure research tools, venoms have time and time again unlocked many neurophysiological and pharmacological secrets[54]. A Melbourne-based company, M.C.M. Biolabs Pty Ltd, has already recognised the benefits of snake venoms and their components and is marketing them within Australia and internationally. Fractions from both Tiger Snake venom 'Tigocoagulase' and Taipan venom 'Taipocoagulase' can be used for assaying blood clotting enzymes. A fraction from Mulga Snake venom 'Anticoagulant K.B.' is proving interesting as an anticoagulant.

PART TWO

SNAKE-BITE MANAGEMENT

Chapter 6
CLINICAL DIAGNOSIS

History

A definite history of snake bite, occasionally including an accurate identification of the offending snake, is often given by the patient. Snake handlers and herpetologists, when bitten, normally give informative histories. On other occasions there is no history of the snake bite. Many victims are children and for various reasons they may wish to hide the fact that they have been bitten by a snake. Parents and doctors should never disregard a history of snake bite from a child[60, 61]. Adults occasionally give false histories of snake bite. There is a common association between heavy alcohol intake and snake bite and this may complicate the diagnosis. The patient may be seriously ill, even unconscious, and only the very alert physician will consider snake bite in his differential diagnosis[62].

In most regions of Australia there are a number of poisonous snakes which, to the untrained observer, often appear similar. For this reason it is extremely difficult and hazardous to identify from the victim's story which

164

venomous snake is involved. Colour alone is an uncertain guide. For instance, in South Australia's Eyre Peninsula region, the Mulga Snake causes confusion in identification because it is often very dark, even black, and in fact it belongs to the Black Snake family. Where monovalent antivenoms are to be used, positive identification of the snake is essential.

A trained herpetologist is an important member of the team for the initial identification and treatment of snake bite[33]. All hospital casualty departments would do well to make arrangements so that they can readily contact a herpetologist in an emergency. Improved venom detection kits, being developed by the Commonwealth Serum Laboratories, may overcome snake identification problems in the future. The real advantage of these kits will be to decrease the need to use large volumes of polyvalent antivenoms[89].

Local reaction

Australia's venomous snakes, unlike many overseas poisonous snakes, produce insignificant proteolytic enzymes and so their bites produce minimal local reaction. It is not uncommon for there to be no local reaction, no pain, bruising, or swelling. Nevertheless, in the authors' experience, all patients seriously envenomated by poisonous snakes did have some local reaction at the bite site. (See photographs, page 79.)

Fairley in 1929 reviewed 281 snake bites and of these 159 (57%) were on the lower limb; twenty-one on the toes; fifty on the feet; eighty-three on the legs; and five on the thigh or knee[1]. Of the other 122 persons, 42% had been bitten on the upper extremity; the fingers seventy-two times; the hands seventeen; the forearm twenty-one and the upper arm on eight occasions. Of the remaining bites, two were on the body, one on the neck, and one on the face.

Venomous snakes have fangs, but fang marks may not be visible. On occasions, venomous snakes do not bite but scratch[60]. The bite may be indicated by a laceration[64], one or many puncture marks, or a small abrasion. A semicircular row of teeth marks may indicate a bite by a non-

165

venomous snake, but multiple bites by venomous snakes can be confusing.

Severe local reactions do occur and have been reported, particularly following Mulga Snake bites[64, 65]. The digit or limb may be very painful, grossly swollen, and the skin blue, motley, or white. If swelling is very severe, gangrene may follow secondary to inadequate tissue perfusion or blood flow, but this is most uncommon.

For definite effective envenomation the snake needs to grip with its jaws. This is more likely to occur when the victim is a child but may result where an adult is drunk, asleep, or irresponsibly handling a venomous snake. There are occasional reports of snakes, usually a Tiger Snake, 'gripping like a bull dog'. Taipans and Death Adders have more effective biting mechanisms because they possess lengthy fangs. Copperhead and Tiger Snakes possess fangs of some 3 mm while the Brown Snake has the smallest fangs of all the major deadly snakes. Another point of interest is that snakes usually only strike once; but an exception to this rule is the Taipan, which may attack repeatedly[66].

Systemic signs

Systemic signs of envenomation may be acute or delayed. Effective bites usually produce obvious problems within twenty minutes and certainly two hours. However, delayed onset of serious illness may occur, particularly where first aid treatment has been effective in slowing lymphatic movement. Some patients have been discharged from hospital only to be readmitted several hours later, very ill. In the past, victims who received no treatment and died, nearly always lived seven hours but rarely longer than twenty-four hours.

Common early signs and symptoms following an effective venomous snake bite are nausea, vomiting, sweating, and headache. Hypotension or low blood pressure may be profound and can occur within minutes. Pain and swelling of local lymph nodes is common and a definite sign of systemic envenomation. An anaphylactic reaction or allergic reaction to the actual venom has been

HE SAYS THE SNAKE BIT
HIM, THEN SWALLOWED HIM.

reported and this may be lethal. Allergic reactions to the venom are more likely to occur in people who are bitten frequently, such as herpetologists[67].

Motor nerve blockade, resulting in muscular weakness, is the major action of the venom. There are two major neurotoxins which both act peripherally at the neuromuscular junction; one presynaptically and the other postsynaptically. Progressively, ptosis or drooping eyelids, diplopia or double vision, dysphagia or swallowing difficulties, and then the insidious onset of diaphragmatic paralysis which leads to respiratory failure, occur. Paralysis of the tongue and palate may precipitate death from respiratory obstruction.

Other systemic signs of snake bite such as coagulation defects (bleeding effect), coagulant activity (clotting effect), and myolytic action (muscle destruction), are less common. Rhabdomyolysis (striated muscle destruction) is thought to be partly due to the presynaptic neurotoxin damaging the skeletal muscles. The patient's urine may turn red from haemoglobinuria before signs of paralysis occur. Bleeding may occur due to hypofibrinogenaemia because prothrombin is converted to thrombin. The thrombin in turn converts fibrinogen to fibrin.

Sensory signs are uncommon following snake bite but can occur. A 24-year-old male bitten by a Kreffts Black Tiger Snake and treated at the Whyalla Hospital lost his taste reception for two months.

Chapter 7
FIRST AID TREATMENT OF SNAKE BITE

> *In practical terms, venom movement can be effec-*
> *tively delayed for long periods by the application*
> *of a firm crepe bandage to the length of the bitten*
> *limb combined with immobilisation by a splint.*
> *Pressure alone or immobilisation alone did not*
> *delay venom movement.*
>
> S. K. Sutherland, 1979[68]

The optimal first aid treatment of snake bite is the immediate application of a firm broad pressure bandage to the bitten area and if possible to the length of the limb. The limb must also be kept still and immobilised by a splint[69]. Clothing or towels can be made into makeshift bandages and a newspaper used for a splint.

For research, Sutherland used an experimental model of an adult monkey restricted in a well-padded frame. He showed that following the injection of Tiger Snake (*Notechis scutatus*) venom into a limb, which was immobilised and compressed, only low levels of circulating venom resulted. The reason for the low plasma levels of venom appeared to be due to immobilising the venom by compressing lymphatics at the bite site and reducing lymph flow. It is also possible that it is due to compression of superficial veins. The pressure used during the experiment was 55 mm mercury and this is equivalent to applying a firm bandage to a sprained ankle. Both crude venom and neurotoxin levels were measured. Snake venom is usually injected subcutaneously and the lymphatics are largely responsible for the venom's absorption. First aid measures aim to decrease and slow down central lymphatic movement.

The victim should rest, not walk around, and should be transferred to hospital with minimal delay. If possible bring transport to the patient rather than vice versa. In

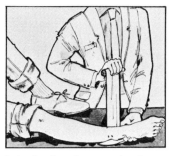

1 Apply a broad pressure bandage over bite site.

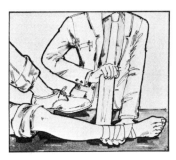

2 Apply bandage firmly.

3 Extend bandage as high as possible.

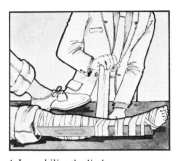

4 Immobilise the limb.

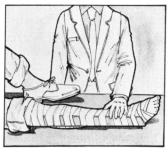

5 Limb immobilised with pressure bandage in place.

remote areas aerial transport and medical retrieval teams should always be considered[33]. Snake identification and early hospital notification are valuable adjuncts to therapy.

During transport hypotension (low blood pressure) and collapse may occur. For this reason it is best to position the patient lying down during transport. Also, if the patient does collapse, his blood pressure and circulation can be improved by raising his legs. It is essential that the victim's airway be maintained and safeguarded. If paralysis is rapid and breathing ceases, mouth to mouth ventilation, applied by untrained personnel in a moving car, will probably be ineffective. In this case the car must be stopped and ventilation attempted with the patient lying on the ground. Help should be fetched and an ambulance with trained first aiders, if possible including a medical team with antivenom supplies, brought to the patient.

Incising and excising snake bite is absolutely contra-indicated[70, 71]. There is no evidence to show that incising snake bites is of any use and clearly it runs the risk of damaging tissues. Recently it was reported in the Australian Press that the Minister of Business and Consumer Affairs, Mr Garland, had banned the sale of snake-bite kits that advocated potentially dangerous methods of treating snake bite, such as excising bitten areas and the use of arterial tourniquets. 'Most such kits consist of unsterile blades, tourniquets and irritant chemicals. They, and the instructions accompanying them, belong to the dark days of the pre-antivenom era.' Cryotherapy and placing the bitten limb in ice are also contraindicated. Alcohol, food, and drugs which depress respiration, should not be given.

Sutherland has shown that the use of arterial tourniquets is impractical because even short usage causes intense distress[72]. He points out that when tourniquets are released there is a surge of blood into the limb causing reflex hyperaemia which results in a rapid central movement of the venom. Although ischaemic damage may occur, to the authors' knowledge it has never been reported.

Tourniquets do reduce the central movement of the lymphatics; arterial tourniquets very effectively but venous tourniquets in an uncertain manner[73]. Venous tourniquets will limit venous and lymphatic return, but venous congestion and discomfort in the limb will result. Although increased lymphatic production does occur, lymphatic stasis can be accomplished.

Many snake bites would not occur if adequate prophylactic measures and greater caution were taken. In snake country always wear protective clothing including long trousers and boots. Avoid long grass and at night time use a torch when walking about in the bush. Cut grass around houses and playgrounds and clear away rubbish. Most important, children should be taught to leave snakes alone. When travelling in remote areas a radio transmitter is valuable for many reasons, including medical communication[74].

The question is often asked, 'We are going for a holiday in the country; should we take antivenom with us?' It is a calculated risk but usually antivenom should not be taken for a number of reasons. It is expensive, needs to be kept in a refrigerator, and if used should be given intravenously with resuscitation equipment and drugs available to treat anaphylaxis if it occurs.

Chapter 8
HOSPITAL TREATMENT

The essence of proper treatment of snake envenomation is simple — give the appropriate antivenom in adequate amounts by the correct route without unnecessary delay.

Editorial, Med. J. Aust.[75]

On admission to hospital the patient may be severely ill, moderately unwell, or show no signs or symptoms at all. Particularly where first aid treatment has been effective, initially it may be difficult to tell how seriously envenomated the patient is. For clinical and medico-legal reasons it is important that hospitals all have well defined policies on the management of snake bite[76].

Severely ill patients

No time should be wasted in establishing an intravenous line, checking resuscitation drugs and equipment, and

I'VE BROUGHT THE SNAKE THAT BIT ME, WITH ME, SO YOU CAN IDENTIFY IT.

giving the antivenom. The patient's airway and breathing must be observed, supported and, if necessary, controlled. Airway obstruction and respiratory failure are rapidly lethal unless quickly diagnosed and corrected. On occasions it is necessary to intubate the patient and ventilate him using a respirator. Tracheostomy is contraindicated since bleeding may occur.

The intravenous line is used for drug therapy, to dilute the antivenom, and if necessary to give emergency drugs. Fluids are all given intravenously and not orally until it is clear that the patient will suffer no airway or swallowing difficulties. Normal saline or 5 per cent dextrose are useful to dilute the antivenom and this is strongly recommended. The patient can be started on oxygen therapy.

Prior to giving antivenom, patients should be premedicated with adrenaline[77] and 5 ml of blood should be taken for snake identification purposes. Adrenaline is the drug of choice to protect against, and for the treatment of, severe anaphylactic reactions[78, 79, 80]. Adrenaline can be given subcutaneously or intramuscularly in a dose of 0·3 ml of 1 in 1000 solution. I have used 0·3 mg of adrenaline, diluted ten times, intravenously for adults; and Sutherland recommends a subcutaneous prophylactic injection before starting the antivenom[5]. If anaphylaxis or serum sickness is likely, steroids (e.g. hydrocortisone 100 mg) intravenously are indicated. Serious reactions are more common where there has been prior sensitisation to horse protein. A non-sedating antihistamine is recommended and it is my practice to give promethazine HCl 25–50 mg intravenously or intramuscularly. (See photograph, page 79.)

All patients with systemic signs of envenomation should be given antivenom intravenously in sufficient amounts to neutralise the venom[81]. The antivenom must be given intravenously because of its large volume (polyvalent is over 40 ml) and because absorption via the subcutaneous and intramuscular routes is too slow. The quantity of venom injected is very variable. The content of one ampoule of antivenom is adequate to neutralise the average yield of the snake *in vitro* but not *in vivo*. The dose of antivenom depends on the amount of venom injected and not on the patient's size. Children may need the same dose or more antivenom than adults.

To decrease the risk of anaphylaxis, dilute the antivenom ten times, and inject it slowly over twenty minutes. In extreme emergencies antivenom can be given more rapidly. The patient must be carefully monitored, preferably in the Intensive Care area, for signs of anaphylaxis or muscle paralysis. If signs or symptoms of envenomation recur or persist another ampoule of antivenom is indicated. Following the release of the tourniquet or compression bandages rapid worsening of the patient's condition may result. More antivenom and effective first aid measures should once again be implemented[82].

'No patient is too ill to receive antivenom and even those with the most severe paralysis may recover[83].'

Australian antivenoms may be effective even when given to moribund patients and a number of case reports vividly illustrate this[60, 83]. It is true that some American medical text books state that antivenom has to be given early but American snake venoms commonly cause massive local necrosis (tissue death). Necrosis occurs rapidly and clearly no amount of antivenom can reverse this. However, Australian venoms are quite different and cause minimal local damage but are strongly neurotoxic.

Only when the identification of the offending snake is definite should monovalent antivenom be used. In 80 per cent of cases identification is not positive and so antivenom is selected on a geographical basis.

State	Appropriate antivenom	Initial dose
Tasmania	Tiger Snake	6000 units
Victoria	Tiger Snake	3000 units
	Brown Snake	1000 units
New South Wales Queensland South Australia Western Australia	Polyvalent snake antivenom	Contents of one ampoule
Papua New Guinea	Polyvalent snake antivenom	Contents of one ampoule

Table 8.1   *Antivenom where identity of snake is unknown*[84, 85]

Where the snake has been postively identified by an expert or by a venom detection kit the appropriate monovalent antivenom is indicated.

Concern about acute anaphylaxis and serum sickness are the two main reasons why doctors occasionally hesitate about giving antivenom. However, as will be discussed later in the section on antivenoms, if patients are premedicated with adrenaline and promethazine HCl and the antivenom diluted, serious reactions are unlikely. Fears about antivenom are largely unfounded and are a hangover of the past when they were far less pure. The real danger today is that antivenom occasionally is not given at all, or that it is given too late and in inadequate amounts.

Victims should always be observed for twenty-four hours[86] because there are reports of patients being seen and discharged from hospital, only to be readmitted some hours later in a moribund state. The patient should be nursed like a head injury and examined hourly. The patient's tetanus immunisation status should be checked and if the wound is dirty, antibiotics are recommended. Pain relief is normally not required but if pain is very severe and opiates used, respiratory depression must be very carefully watched for.

Snake	Appropriate antivenom	Initial dose
Tiger Snake	Tiger Snake	3000 units
Tasmanian Tiger Snake	Tiger Snake	6000 units
Chappell Island Tiger Snake	Tiger Snake	12000 units
Death Adder	Death Adder	6000 units
Taipan	Taipan	12000 units
Inland Taipan (Fierce Snake)	Taipan	12000 units
Copperhead	Tiger Snake	3000–6000 units*
Brown Snake	Brown Snake	1000 units
Dugite	Brown Snake	1000 units
Western Brown Snake (Gwardar)	Brown Snake	1000 units
Peninsula Brown Snake	Brown Snake	1000 units
Black Snake	Tiger Snake or Black Snake	3000 units 6000 units
Mulga Snake	Black Snake	18000 units
Rough-scaled Snake	Tiger Snake	3000 units

*6000 units Tasmania[26]

Table 8.2 *Antivenom where identity of snake is known*

The most common cause of death following snake bite is respiratory failure. Death from renal failure or bleeding diathesis is less common. For seriously ill patients, supportive measures as well as giving antivenom may be needed. If renal failure results and renal output ceases, peritoneal dialysis and haemodialysis may be life saving[87, 88]. When coagulation defects occur, correct therapy, certainly in rural areas, is to give more antivenom and to transport the patient to a major medical centre.

Fresh blood should not be administered or massive clotting and thrombosis may follow.

Avoidable deaths from snake bite continue to occur and the reasons remain unaltered from those listed by Sutherland in 1975[81].

1. Antivenom is withheld despite clear evidence of envenomation.

2. The wrong antivenom is administered: occasionally when the snake has been mistakenly identified.

3. The appropriate antivenom is given but the quantity is inadequate.

4. The dose of antivenom is not repeated when the signs and symptoms of envenomation persist or recur.

5. The victim is not under medical surveillance for an adequate period.

Chapter 9
LABORATORY TESTS

Laboratory tests are important in the management of suspected or definite snake bite. Often such tests will demonstrate changes due to envenomation very soon after the bite has occurred. Deterioration in the patient's clinical condition may even be preceded by abnormal laboratory results.

Identification samples must be collected prior to giving the patient any antivenom. Specimens should include 5 ml of blood, 5 ml of urine, a saline swab of the bite site, and any stained clothing[77]. Following communication with Commonwealth Serum Laboratories personnel in Melbourne (telephone (03) 389 1911) the specimens should be urgently despatched, packed in dry ice to keep them frozen.

Radioimmunoassay can accurately detect and quantitate venom and also identify the poisonous snake. It is particularly useful to confirm or eliminate envenomation as a diagnosis in difficult cases or postmortem studies. How-

Snake venom detection kit manufactured by Commonwealth Serum Laboratories

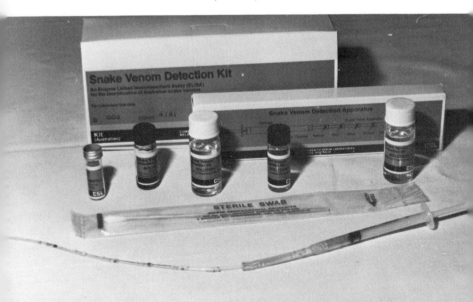

ever, radioimmunoassay is of little benefit for the immediate management of snake bite because all facilities for this service are located in Melbourne. Also, false positive results can occur; but these can be eliminated by dilution of the specimen.

In 1979 the Commonwealth Serum Laboratories distributed 600 experimental snake venom detection kits for evaluation[89]. The kits gave qualitative results in about thirty minutes when used by untrained personnel. These kits, because of the time delay and their complexity, have proved only partially successful. Recently, however, faster and simpler kits have been produced by the Commonwealth Serum Laboratories, greatly simplifying identification problems of snake bite. The snake venom detection apparatus consists of six glass tubes joined by plastic tubing. A positive result produces a colour change from yellow to intense purple.

Recommended laboratory investigations

1. *Blood and Serum*
   1 Freeze 5 ml of blood.
   2 Bleeding and clotting studies. Fibrin degradation products.
   3 Fibrinogen levels.
   4 Multiple biochemical analysis. Enzymes, electrolytes, blood urea.
   5 Group and screen for antibodies.

2. *Urine*
   1 Freeze 5 ml.
   2 Hourly output.
   3 Haemoglobin.
   4 Myoglobin.
   5 Red blood cells.

3. *Bite Site*
   1 Freeze saline swab.

Bleeding and clotting studies are a sensitive guide to the patient's condition and if altered should be repeated frequently. If inadequate antivenom has been given in the presence of severe envenomation the activated partial thromboplastin time (PTTK) is prolonged, the fibrinogen level drops, the fibrin degradation products increase, and the platelet count diminishes. The correct treatment of altered bleeding and clotting studies is more antivenom, not fibrinogen, fresh blood, heparin or epsilon amino caproic acid.

Haemoglobin in the urine indicates lysis of red blood cells. Red blood cells in the urine is a pointer towards a bleeding and clotting problem developing. Lysis of muscle cells can be diagnosed when myoglobin is found in the urine.

In my experience very high serum enzymes are common, particularly serum creatinine kinase. This may be due to muscle damage from the venom but often results from ischaemia secondary to the tourniquet or from the patient exercising prior to collection of the blood sample.

Chapter 10
VENOMS

Australian snake venoms are among the deadliest in the world and are particularly rich in potent neurotoxins[90]. The venoms are a specially developed form of saliva consisting of proteins, many of which are enzymes. The venoms have a dual purpose of immobilising the prey and then assisting with its digestion[5, 26].

The main pharmacological actions of Australian snake venoms are as follows:

Neurotoxins

These act peripherally at the neuromuscular junction causing paralysis of the voluntary muscles. There are at least two major neurotoxins. In severe cases, death is caused by asphyxiation and respiratory failure due to paralysis secondary to the effects of the neurotoxins.

Haemotoxins

Haemolytic venoms destroy red blood cells and this results in intravascular haemolysis. The resulting haemoglobin in the urine (haemoglobinuria) may cause the urine to turn red.

Coagulants

Coagulants cause the blood to clot within the blood vessels.

Cytotoxins

Destroy the cells of the blood or those of any other tissue with which they come into contact. They include cardiotoxins and myotoxins.

Anticoagulants

Impede the clotting of the blood and this may result in bleeding. Blood in the urine (haematuria) causes the urine to turn red.

Hyaluronidase activity

An enzyme in Australian snake venoms which accelerates the onset of systemic toxic effects of the venom by facilitating its movement in the tissue[11, 40]. Hyaluronidase is also called the 'spreading factor'.

One method used to study the components of different venoms is electrophoresis. A pattern is produced by placing the venom between charged plates in a gel. Each component has a different electric affinity for the positive and negative poles. The venom proteins separate according to their charge density and are revealed as bands on the gel by a general protein stain. For example, in the photograph below, the patterns 1 to 9 were produced by: 1. Inland Taipan; 2. Common Brown Snake; 3. Taipan; 4. Sea Snake (*Enhydrina schistosa*); 5. Common Tiger Snake; 6. Western Tiger Snake; 7. Chappell Island Tiger Snake; 8. Western Brown Snake; 9. Common Death Adder.

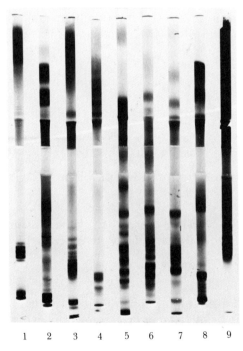

Electrophoretic patterns of nine snake venoms showing distinctions between them. (Courtesy Dr S. Sutherland, Head of Immunology Research, Commonwealth Serum Laboratories.)

Chapter 11
HISTORY OF ANTIVENOMS

Earliest reference to snake-bite treatment goes back to 1600 B.C. to the ancient papyri from old Egypt where prescriptions have been found for snake and insect bites. Leek, garlic, and onion juices were popular remedies but hardly successful antidotes. In medieval times goats and pigs were thought to have some special significance in snake-bite cures. Goats' cheese, rancid goats' butter, and pig lard were applied to the bite area or taken internally. Excreta and urine were used as snake-bite cures. Excreta was applied to the bite, or the victim was buried up to the neck in fresh manure[91, 92].

A native antidote from Ceylon recommended that special pills be soaked in urine and then applied to the incised bite area. Care was taken to ensure the urine was free from venereal disease. In severe cases the pills were administered through the nostrils. Famous snake doctors of Asia Minor cured snake bite by placing their fingers directly on the bite or spitting on the wound. In extreme cases they would place their naked bodies on the bite[92].

Primitive medicines were based on the 'eye for an eye' principle. The body of an asp, preferably the offender, or the bowels of a snake were eaten or applied to the wound. The Hindus even believed that if the victim bit the head off the offending snake the venom would be neutralised[92].

In the mid-nineteenth century there were some weird and absurd remedies for snake bite. One such treatment was the fabled snake stone of Asia. Directions for its application instructed the user to cut the bite in the shape of an X until blood oozed out and then to apply the stone, which remained in the wound for two to three hours. When the stone fell off, it was wiped and left in milk for half an hour. Then the stone was rinsed, dried, and applied again. The stone was supposed to withdraw the venom from the wound. Perhaps not quite so bizarre were the snake-bite tablets and herbal balls which were applied to the bite or eaten[93].

There were many other bizarre, cruel, and drastic treatments, but probably the most dangerous occurred after gun powder was invented. After incision, gun powder was sprinkled into the wound and exploded. Undoubtedly there were some catastrophic results from this method[92].

Alcohol was added to the seemingly endless list of cures. In Australia and America massive doses of alcohol have been used for snake-bite cure. In America a victim who received large quantities of whisky after a Rattle-snake bite recovered so remarkably that the next day he went searching for another Rattle-snake to bite him[92].

Up to 1880 no cure had been found for snake bite. However, all of the herbal remedies, live and dead animal cures, and snake stones were proved to be useless. It was shortly after this that a breakthrough occurred. An American, H. Sewall, in 1887 found that animals injected with sub-lethal doses of Rattle-snake venom gradually built up an immunity to the venom. The French at the Pasteur Institute who had previously learnt the significance of antibodies, extended the American experiments and found that animals could be immunised with the blood of another animal which had undergone gradual venom immunity therapy. From this, the idea of using another animal's blood as an antidote for snake bite evolved. Snakes were milked of their venom and horses were used to produce the antidotes. But the early hopes of an antivenom suitable for all snakes were not realised. Researchers found that the antivenoms produced were only specific as a cure against the snakes used for milking[92].

In Australia the deadliest terrestrial snakes in the world occur and in the 1920s the Commonwealth Serum Laboratories under Dr C. H. Kellaway undertook a major project in developing antidotes for Australia's deadly snakes. To find a cure for Australian snake bite, Tiger Snake antivenom was the first objective. To produce it Dr Kellaway organised the snake men of the day to collect snakes, and milk them, and he taught them how to store venom. This allowed a few of them to earn a living from snakes and thus devote time to their interest[1, 91].

Initially, small doses of the venom were injected into horses. Gradually the doses were increased until the horses could withstand doses that would kill many hundreds of non-treated horses. After a period, the horses were bled and large quantities of blood collected. Plasma extracted from the blood contained the serum used for Tiger Snake antivenom. In 1929 an effective antidote against Tiger Snake bite was commercially prepared. In addition, some cross protection against other snake bites was afforded by this antivenom. Since allergies could occur from horse serum, the increased dosage required for non-specific bites led to the development of other specific antivenoms for other Australian snakes. In 1955 Taipan antivenom was produced and this was followed by Brown Snake antivenom. In 1959 Death Adder antivenom was developed. Production of a polyvalent antivenom in 1962 gave protection against snake bite from any Australian snake and removed the necessity for identification[91, 94].

Common Cobra (exotic) *Naja naja*	1
King Cobra (exotic) *Ophiophagus hannah*	0·26
Eastern Diamondback Rattle-snake (exotic) *Crotalus adamanteus*	0·06
Common Tiger Snake (native) *Notechis scutatus*	4·25
Taipan (native) *Oxyuranus scutellatus scutellatus*	7·87
Common Brown Snake (native) *Pseudonaja textilis textilis*	12·35
Inland Taipan (native) *Oxyuranus microlepidotus*	49·5

Table 11.1 *Relative toxicity of Australian snakes with overseas snakes* (Figures derived from reference 2)

To put Australian snakes in perspective, some recent work carried out by the Commonwealth Serum Laboratories enables an accurate comparison of the venoms of overseas snakes and Australian snakes. If we choose the venom from the Common Cobra (*Naja naja*) and call its toxicity unity, other venoms will be either more or less toxic.

From the Table it can be seen that compared with the Common Cobra, the Common Tiger Snake is 4·25 times deadlier and the Inland Taipan is almost 50 times deadlier.

Snake bite presents a significant health risk in Australia. Over 200 cases of snake bite requiring antivenom are reported yearly and over the years a number of deaths have occurred. Prior to 1926 the average yearly death rate was about fifteen. In 1976 statistics showed the annual death rate to be about five. However, in 1979 there was only one death in Australia due to snake bite; and up until June 1981 there had been no deaths for two years.

The reduction in death rate since 1926 can be attributed largely to the production of antivenom. Other factors include reductions in snake populations due to environmental pressures and more recently the active role of Dr S. Sutherland (Head of Immunology Research at the Commonwealth Serum Laboratories) in using every opportunity in journals, the media, and medical courses to outline snake-bite treatment management techniques.

The only effective treatment of snake bite in Australia is by the use of an antivenom made by the Commonwealth Serum Laboratories. Hospitals stock specific antivenoms of locally occurring snakes and also polyvalent serum which can be used for any snake bite. Hospitals in Tasmania only require Tiger Snake antivenom. The latest development by the Commonwealth Serum Laboratory is a snake-bite kit that allows rapid identification of the snake venom type when a blood sample is taken from the patient and tested in the kit[95].

Chapter 12
ANTIVENOMS

*It is never too late to administer antivenom, except
when the patient is dead.*

S. K. Sutherland[83]

Antivenom is the only specific treatment of snake bite and
today virtually all snake-bite deaths are due to lack of
adequate correct antivenom. Antivenoms should never be
withheld when there are clear indications for their use.
On occasions, antivenoms may not be available, but
usually where tragedies occur, too little antivenom has
been given, often too late.

Unfortunately, some doctors still believe that antivenoms 'are more dangerous than the disease itself' but
this is not correct. In 1977 Sutherland reviewed all serious
reactions to antivenoms over a fifteen year period and
found no deaths were related to anaphylaxis[96]. More
recently, Sutherland followed up 181 out of 203 (89%)
cases where antivenom was used to treat snake-bite victims
during the twelve-month period from July 1978 to June
1979 and again, there were no deaths[97].

Nevertheless, reactions to antivenom are reasonably
common and this is why patients should be premedicated
with an antihistamine and adrenaline and the antivenom
given diluted. In early days when antivenoms were very
crude preparations and many people had been sensitised
to equine proteins following the use of antisera (e.g. for
tetanus and diphtheria immunisation), severe reactions
were more worrying. Trinca in 1963 noted that a decade
earlier three deaths had occurred from anaphylactic reactions[98]. Since this report, to my knowledge, there has
been no death due to anaphylactic reactions to snake
antivenom in Australia. Today, because reactions are less
severe and less common, it is very wrong to use antivenom
only in desperate situations.

Serum is separated from blood collected from horses at Woodend

To make the antivenom a constant supply of snake venom is required and this is acquired from a number of recognised herpetologists who keep sufficient snakes in captivity and periodically milk them. Most of the dangerous species adapt to captive life and are not upset unduly by fortnightly milkings. Apart from a few traumatic moments while being held behind the neck and forced to bite on to a tightly stretched rubber diaphragm the snakes adapt to captivity, feed well, and will even reproduce if given the right conditions. (See photographs, page 80.)

It is interesting to note that unlike American Rattle-snakes, most Australian snakes can be kept in captivity for years and milked regularly without any deterioration in health. American Rattle-snakes are only milked once for venom used for antivenom production. This is because the venom glands are frequently damaged when milked and second and third milkings often contain blood and cellular material that contaminates the venom.

When milking Australian snakes for venom many snakes of the one species are milked into one container. This venom is dried in a vacuum desiccator before being sent to the Commonwealth Serum Laboratories in Melbourne. The venoms are prepared and then sent to the Laboratories' small farm at Woodend, about eighty kilometres from Melbourne. On the 616-hectare farm about 250 French-bred Percheron horses are regularly injected with venoms from snakes, spiders, and ticks. The snake venom is injected at increasing dosages until the horse has developed sufficient antibodies. The serum is then collected and fractionated. The horse immunoglobulins are purified, concentrated, and standardised to contain a minimal number of units. A unit of antivenom will neutralise 0·01 mg of dried snake venom.

Antivenom should be stored away from the light in a refrigerator between 0°C and 10°C. It should not be frozen and its shelf life is three years. Antivenom is available for hospitals free of charge and is also available for sale to the public.

In Australia all snake-bite antivenoms are of equine origin and contain large volumes of protein. One ampoule of Australian polyvalent antivenom contains more than 40 ml of 17% equine protein. This is greater than any other overseas polyvalent antivenom and also has the highest protein concentration. Such an enormous quantity of antivenom is required because of the potency and yield of Australia's dangerous snakes.

Antivenoms possess considerable anti-complementary activity and it is believed that anaphylactic reactions are due, at least in part, to this activity[99]. The more protein infused the greater the chance of an immediate or a delayed

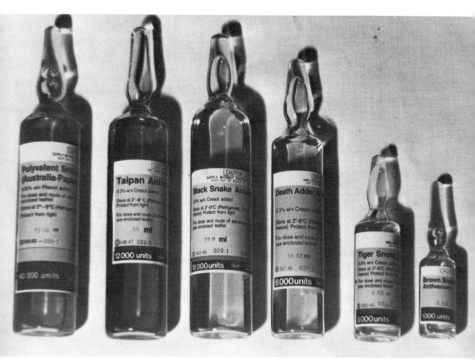

Antivenoms manufactured by Commonwealth Serum Laboratories

reaction. In 1969 Campbell reviewed 61 cases of snake bite treated at the Moresby General Hospital and 28 patients (46%) developed some side effect, including five (8%) who suffered a serious anaphylactic-type reaction[100]. Delayed reactions were more common following large doses of antivenom. Sutherland has reported that 79% of unexpected reactions to antivenom occur following usage of the large volume polyvalent antivenom[97]. In these same series Sutherland noted 13% of patients suffered some untoward effects when given antivenom. Patients receiving polyvalent have a 10% or greater chance of developing a significant delayed reaction. Clearly, where the snake has been accurately identified, it is preferable to use the small volume monovalent antivenom. Severe, acute, and delayed reactions, are more common in older snake-bite victims, suggesting prior exposure to equine protein may be a factor.

190

Antivenom should be given when there are definite signs or symptoms of systemic envenomation. It is likely that all patients who have been effectively bitten by a mature, dangerous, snake will need antivenom. Children become critically ill faster than adults because of their small body weight and because they more frequently have suffered multiple bites. The dose of antivenom for a child is the same as for an adult and that is enough to neutralise the venom.

WHAT! WE BOTH GET THE SAME DOSE OF ANTIVENOM!

Details on how to give antivenom are listed on the package by the Commonwealth Serum Laboratories. The antivenom should be diluted 1 in 10 in saline solution and then slowly infused over twenty minutes. Prior to starting the infusion the patient should receive an anti-histamine, e.g. Phenergan 25–50 mg and subcutaneous adrenaline. Adrenaline is the drug par excellence in reducing anaphylactic shock and the dose in adults is about 0·3 mg. Steroids are recommended for patients likely to develop serum sickness, which includes those persons with a relevant allergic history, asthma sufferers, and those who have received equine protein previously. Wherever possible, it is recommended that antivenom be given by medical personnel in hospital where there are satisfactory facilities for resuscitation. When these precautions are taken, serious reactions to antivenom are unlikely. Preliminary sensitivity tests are not accurate and skin testing with antivenom is not recommended.

When determining the dose of antivenom required the following facts should be kept in mind. The quantity of antivenom in an ampoule is the amount required to neutralise the venom from an 'average yield' milking, *in vitro*. The quantity of venom injected into a snake-bite victim is unknown but may be more than an 'average yield' milking. If five times the quantity of venom has been injected, five ampoules of antivenom would be required. Where delays in using antivenom have occurred, more antivenom may be required. No patient is too ill to receive antivenom.

In 1929 the first national distribution of antivenom took place in Australia. It was an antivenom for the treatment of Tiger Snake bite. Following this other specific mono-valent antivenoms were produced and this culminated in 1962 with the release of polyvalent antivenom for use in Australia and Papua New Guinea. Since the introduction and distribution of polyvalent antivenom it has no longer been essential to identify the snake involved. A number of zoos and herpetologists keep imported snakes and the need to maintain banks of antivenom against these snakes was recently highlighted when a Pygmy Rattle-snake (*Sistrurus miliarius*) bit a herpetologist at Warrnambool[101]. He was flown to Melbourne, given Rattle-snake anti-venom, and following a serious illness, successfully recovered.

Reactions to antivenoms may be immediate or delayed and can be mild to severe. Immediate mild symptoms and signs include pyrexia, rash, sweating, headache, mild bron-chospasm, cough, and vomiting. Severe immediate problems are usually vascular, such as hypotension and collapse, or respiratory, causing bronchospasm and wheez-ing. Patients with delayed mild illnesses complain of urticaria, mild arthralgia, and polylymphadenopathy. However, some patients develop serum sickness and are very ill with pyrexia, joint and muscle pains, and gross urticaria.

GLOSSARY

Anaphylaxis: An exaggerated allergic reaction.
Anterior: Towards the front of the snake.
Arboreal: Tree-living.
Archipelago: A group of small islands.
Arthralgia: Painful joints.

Basking: A term used in a loose sense to describe a snake's behaviour when lying in the direct or diffused sun's rays. Thermoregulation may or may not be taking place.
Bifurcated: Divided into two branches.
Bolus: Soft lump of faecal matter.

Cardiotoxins: Agents having a poisonous effect upon the heart.
Caudal: Tail section of the snake (from the anal scale to the terminal scale).
Cloaca: The common cavity in which the rectum and ureters connect to eject both waste and reproductive matter through a single opening.
Coagulant: A substance which causes blood to clot.
Copulation: Sexual union.
Cytotoxin: A substance having a poisonous effect on cells.

Dentary: Lower jaw bone, housing the mandibular teeth.
Diurnal: Active during daylight hours.
Dorsal: Top surface of the snake.

Ecology: Relationship between snakes and their environment.
Electrophoretic patterns: Patterns produced by applying electric fields to the substance to create dispersion.
Enzyme: A protein that accelerates chemical reactions.

Fibrinogen: A protein that accelerates blood clotting.

Genus: Group of things (snakes) having similar structural characteristics, e.g. *Notechis, Acanthophis, Pseudonaja*, etc.

Gravid: Pregnant.

Haematuria: Blood in the urine.

Haemoglobin: The oxygen-carrying pigment in red blood cells.

Haemolysis: The destruction of red blood cells.

Haemotoxin: A substance poisonous to red blood cells.

Hemipenes: A penis on both sides of tail, directly opposite each other.

Hibernation: An inactive period during colder months of the year.

Hyaluronidase: An enzyme that destroys hyaluronic acid, the cement substance of tissues.

Ischaemia: Deficiency of blood.

Isohyet: A line drawn on a map that links places of equal rainfall.

Jacobsons Organ: A paired organ located in the front of the palate that tests scent molecules transferred by the bifurcated tongue.

Karyotyping: Characteristics of cell nuclei, especially size, form, and chromosome number.

Keeled: A raised ridge on individual scales.

Kinase: Enzymes that catalyse the transfer of energy groups between cells.

Lethal Dose (LD$_{50}$): The dose which results in the death of 50% of test subjects.

Lysis: The destruction of cells.

Mandibular teeth: Teeth on lower dentary bone.

Maxillary: Upper jaw bone housing the fangs, reserve fangs, and the post-maxillary teeth.

Morbidity: Tending towards sickness.

Morphology: Biological forms.

Mortality: Death rate.

Myotoxin: A substance poisonous to muscles.

Necrosis: Death of tissue.

Neurophysiological: Dealing with physiology in relation to nerves.

Neurotoxin: A substance having a poisonous effect on nerves.

Nocturnal: Active at night.

Olfactory: System used for smelling.

Oviparous: Egg laying.

Ovoviviparous: The eggs hatch within the female, or as the egg is laid, or shortly after. The egg has a transparent membrane and lacks the leathery white outer layer as in oviparous snakes.

Palatine: Upper jaw bones at front of mouth. House palatine teeth.

Pharmocological: The study of the preparation, use, and effects of drugs.

Polylymphadenopathy: Multiple enlarged lymph nodes.

Post-maxillary: Teeth behind the fang.

Pterygo-palatine teeth: Teeth behind palatine teeth.

Pyrexia: Fever.

Rhabdomyolysis: Disintegration of striated muscle fibres with excretion of myoglobin in the urine.

Rugose: A wrinkled or rough surface.

Samphire: Low coastal salt-tolerant succulent plant.

Scalation: Arrangement of scales on the snake.

Scales: Thin horny overlapping plates protecting the snake's skin.

Sloughing: Process of shedding skin.

Species: A subdivision of a genus where a group of things (snakes) have common characteristics, e.g.,

Genus	species	sub-species
Notechis	*scutatus*	
Notechis	*ater*	*niger*

Subcaudal: Under tail (subcaudal scales are those on the underside of the tail).

Thermoregulation: Control of body temperature.
Toxicity: Degree of poisonousness.
Trachea: Duct for breathing air. Located forward in the bottom jaw in snakes.
Trematode: Flat worms living as parasites in or on snakes.

Ureters: Ducts through which urine passes.
Urticaria: Itching, stinging skin.

Vagina dentis: Fleshy sheath covering the fangs.
Ventral: Refers to the underside of snake.
Vipers: Family of snakes, Viperidae, not represented in Australia. These snakes have the ability to rotate their fangs back after closing their mouths.

REFERENCES

1   Fairley, N. H. 'The present position of snake-bite and the snake bitten in Australia.' *Med. J. Aust.*, 9 March 1929, pp. 296–313.
2   Broad, A. J., Sutherland, S. K. and Coulter, A. R. 'The lethality in mice of dangerous Australian and other snake venoms.' *Toxicon.*, 17, 1979, pp. 664–67.
3   Australia's Most Dangerous Snakes. Queensland Museum Colour Transparencies, No. 2.
4   Sutherland, S. K. *et al.* 'Australia's potentially most venomous snake: *Parademansia microlepidotus.*' *Med. J. Aust.*, vol. 1, 1978, pp. 288–89.
5   Sutherland, S. K. 'Treatment of arachnid poisoning in Australia.' *Aust. Family Physician*, April 1976, pp. 305–12.
6   Morgan, F. G., Director of Commonwealth Serum Laboratories. 'The venom of *Notechis scutatus* variety *niger* (Reevesby Island).' *Proc. Roy. Soc. Victoria*, 50(2): pp. 303–413, Melbourne, 1937.
7   Worrell, E. *Reptiles of Australia.* Angus and Robertson, Sydney, 1963.
8   Softly, A. 'Necessity for Perpetration of a Venomous Snake.' *Biological Conservation*, vol. 4, no. 1, Applied Science Publishers, Great Britain, October, 1971, pp 40–42.
9   Mirtschin, P. J. Personal milking records. May 1980.
10 Howell, E. and Naylor, L. Personal communication re milking records, 1981.
11 'Snake-bite and its Treatment in Animals in Australia.' Commonwealth Serum Laboratories Veterinary Handbook, 1979.
12 Lawton, D. (Taronga Park Zoo) Milking records, 1980.
13 Fairley, N. H. 'Venom yields in Australian Poisonous snakes.' Symposium on snake-bite. *Med. J. Aust.*, 16 March 1929, pp. 336–44.
14 Pollitt, C. C. 'Studies of venom and blood of the Eastern

Small-eyed snake, *Crytophis nigrescens* (Gunther).' Melbourne Herpetological Symposium abstracts, May 1980, p. 6.

[15] Kellaway, C. H. 'Symposium on snake-bite. Preliminary note on the venom of *Pseudechis guttatus*.' *Med. J. Aust.*, 23 March 1929, pp. 372–77.

[16] Romer, A. S. *Osteology of the reptiles*. University of Chicago Press, Chicago, 1956.

[17] Cogger, H. Letter to P. J. Mirtschin, 18 December 1980.

[18] Shine, R. 'Habits, Diets and Sympatry in Snakes: A Study from Australia.' *Canadian Journal Zoology*, 55, 1977, pp. 1118–28.

[19] Waite, E. R. *Reptiles and Amphibians of South Australia*. Government Printer, Adelaide, 1928.

[20] Shine, R. 'Reproduction in Australian Elapid Snakes. 1. Testicular Cycles and Mating Seasons.' *Aust. J. Zoology*, 25, 1977, pp. 647–53.

[21] Rankin, P. R. 'Mating of Wild Red-bellied Black Snakes *Pseudechis porphyriacus* (Shaw).' *Herpetofauna*, 8(1), February 1976, pp. 10–15.

[22] Shine, R. 'Growth rate and sexual maturation in six species of Australian elapid snakes.' *Herpetologica*, 34(1), March 1978, pp. 73–79.

[23] Mirtschin, P. J. Field Notes. Records of the Reevesby Island Tiger Snake, 1977–80.

[24] Schwaner, T. S.A. Museum. Personal communication 1980.

[25] Gow, G. F. *Snakes of Australia*. Angus and Robertson, Sydney, 1976.

[26] 'Venomous bites and stings: Use of antivenom.' C.S.L. Medical Handbook, Chapter 11, 1979.

[27] Giddings, S. 'Some Notes on Trematode Infestation in Tiger Snakes in South Australia.' *Herpetofauna*, vol. 10, no. 1, August 1978, pp. 7–8.

[28] Mirtschin, P. J. 'Tick infestation of Black Tiger snakes and Peninsular Brown snakes on the Coffin Bay Peninsular, South Australia.' Unpublished, sent to N.P.W.S., S.A., and S.A. Museum, 1974.

[29] Mirtschin, P. J. Whyalla Fauna Park Records, 1977.

30 Sutherland, S. Personal communication regarding toxicity of Kreffts Tiger Snake, 1980.

31 Mirtschin, P. J. Fang-length of Kangaroo Island Tiger Snake road kill. (Personal field notes) September 1980.

32 Mirtschin, P. J. and Hudson, P. Scalation Records from Juvenile Reevesby Island Black Tiger Snakes Born 14 March 1980. Private records. Sent to S.A. Museum.

33 Davis, R., Fennell, P. and Mirtschin, P. 'Poisonous Snakes of South Australia's Eyre Region—Identification and Treatment. A Co-ordinated Approach.' *Whyalla Press*, Whyalla, S.A., 1979.

34 Worrell, E. *Song of the Snake*. Angus and Robertson, Sydney, 1958.

35 Gillam, M. W. 'The genus *Pseudonaja (Serpentes: Elapidae)* in the Northern Territory.' Territory Parks and Wildlife Commission Research Bulletin, No. 1, June 1979.

36 Storr, G. M. *Dangerous Snakes of Western Australia*. Western Australian Museum, 1979.

37 Pamphlet accompanying the venom detection kit. Commonwealth Serum Laboratories, 1980.

38 Covacevich, J., McDowell, S. and Tanner, C. 'Relationship of the Taipan, *Oxyuranus scutellatus* and small scaled snake, *Oxyuranus microlepidotus*.' *Proc. Herp. Symposium*, Melbourne Zoo, May 1980 (in press).

39 Charles N. Personal communication regarding general aspects of the Taipan, 1979.

40 Broad, A. J., Sutherland, S. K., Tanner, C. and Covacevich, J. 'Electrophoretic, enzyme and preliminary toxicity studies of the venom of the small-scaled snake: *Parademansia microlepidota (Serpente: Elapidae)*, with additional data on its distribution.' *Mem. Qls. Mus.*, 19(3): 319–29, pls. 1–2, 1979.

41 Covacevich, J. and Wombey, J. 'Recognition of *Parademansia Microlepidotus* (McCoy).' *Proc. Royal Soc. Qld.*, 87: 29–32, pls 1–2, 1976.

42 Mirtschin, P. Report on visit to Goyders Lagoon. April 1980. (Unpublished. Sent to S.A. Museum, N.P.W.S., S.A.).

43 Fohlman, J. 'Comparison of two highly toxic Australian snake venoms: The Taipan (*Oxyuranus scutellatus*) and Fierce Snake (*Parademansia microlepidotus*).' *Toxicon.*, 17, 1979, pp. 170–72.

44 Cogger, H. G. *Reptiles of Australia.* A. H. & A. W. Reed, Sydney, 1975.

45 Mirtschin, P. J. Records Whyalla Fauna Park on King Brown Snake feeding, 1977–80.

46 Records from the Queen Victoria Museum and Art Gallery, Tasmania.

47 Bredl, J. Personal communication on Pale-headed snake, 1981.

48 'Trafficking in Fauna in Australia.' Second Report of the House of Representatives Standing Committee on Environment and Conservation, September, 1976, Parliament of the Commonwealth of Australia. Australian Government Publishing Service, Canberra.

49 'The Status of Endangered Australian Wildlife.' Proceedings of the Centenary Symposium of the Royal Zoological Society of South Australia, Adelaide, 21–23 September 1978.

50 Bowen, B. K. Letter from Department of Fisheries and Wildlife, Western Australia, 4 August 1980.

51 Letters from all National Parks Departments regarding protection and status of dangerous snakes, 1980.

52 Bayly, C. P. 'Observations on the food of the feral cat (*Felis catus*) in an arid environment.' *South Australian Naturalist*, 51(2), December 1976, pp. 22–24.

53 Kellaway, C. H. 'Venom of *Notechis scutatus.*' *Med. J. Aust.*, 16 March 1929.

54 Sutherland, S. K. 'Treatment of snake-bite in Australia and P.N.G.' *Aust. Nurses J.*, 10(2), August 1980, pp. 46–52.

55 Covacevich, J. and Archer, M. 'The Distribution of the Cane Toad, *Bufo marinus*, in Australia and its Effect on Indigenous Vetebrates.' *Mem. Qld. Museum*, 1975.

56 Serventy, V. *Australia—A Continent in Danger*, Andre Deutsch Limited, London, 1966.

57 Bredl, J. Personal communication re Tiger Snake deaths on Murray River during flooding, 1979.

58 Hughes, G. and Wilson, F. Personal communication re flooding of Diamantina River, 1980.

59 Mirtschin, P. J. Visit to the Strzelecki Track by the Western Herpetology Group, September 1977. Report unpublished, sent to N.P.W.S., S.A. Museum.

60 Gaynor, B. 'An unusual snake bite story.' *Med. J. Aust.*, vol. 2, 1977, pp. 191–92.

61 Sutherland, S. K., Coulter, A. R. 'Three instructive cases of Tiger snake (*Notechis scutatus*) envenomation and how a radioimmunoassay proved the diagnosis.' *Med. J. Aust.*, vol. 2, 1977, pp. 177–80.

62 Sutherland, S. K. 'Need for improved management of snake bite.' *Impulse*, October 1975, pp. 1–3.

63 Sutherland, S. K. and Coulter, A. R. 'Snake bite: Detection of venom by radioimmunoassay.' *Med. J. Aust.*, vol. 2, 12 November 1977, pp. 683–84.

64 Vines, A. 'Severe local reaction to bite of King Brown snake.' *Med. J. Aust.*, vol. 1, 17 June 1978, p. 657.

65 Campbell, C. H. 'Fatal case of mulga (*Pseudechis australis*) snake bite.' *Med. J. Aust.*, vol. 1, 1969, p. 426.

66 Sutherland, S. K., *et al.* 'Rapid death of a child after Taipan bite.' *Med. J. Aust.*, vol. 1, 9 February 1980, p. 136.

67 Sutherland, S. K. Letter. *Med. J. Aust.*, vol. 1, 17 June 1978, p. 657.

68 Sutherland, S. K., *et al.* 'Rationalisation of first aid measures for Elapid snake-bite.' *Lancet*, 27 January 1979, pp. 183–86.

69 The National Health and Medical Research Council 'Treatment of snake bite.' *Med. J. Aust.*, vol. 2, 8 September 1979, p. 257.

70 The Australian Resuscitation Council. *The management of snake bite*, 1978.

71 Sutherland, S. K. *First aid for snake bite in Australia.* Commonwealth Serum Laboratories publication, Melbourne, 1979.

72 First aid for snake bite in Australia. Editorial, *Med. J. Aust.*, vol. 1, 19 May 1979, pp. 437–38.

73 Fairley, H. N. 'Criteria for determining the efficacy of ligature in snake bite.' *Med. J. Aust.*, March 1929, pp. 377–94.

74 Sutherland, S. K. 'Snake bite in remote areas.' *Med. J. Aust.*, vol. 6, 2 June 1979, p. 520.

75 'The management of snake bite.' Editorial, *Med. J. Aust.*, vol. 6, 11 February 1978, pp. 137–38.

76 Sullivan, M. J. 'Snake bite in Australia. The problems involved and a protocol for hospital management.' *Anaesth. Intens. Care*, vol. 7, 1979, p. 341.

77 Sutherland, S. K. 'Treatment of snake bite in Australia and Papua New Guinea.' *Aust. Fam. Physician.*, vol. 5, 1976, pp. 272–88.

78 Munro Ford, R. 'The management of acute allergic disease including anaphylaxis.' *Med. J. Aust.*, vol. 1, 12 February 1977, pp. 222–23.

79 Morrow, D. H. and Luther, R. R. 'Anaphylaxis—Aetiology and guidelines for management.' *Anesthesia and Analgesia: Current Researches*, vol. 11, no. 4, July 1976, pp. 494–99.

80 Fisher, M. M. 'The Management of Anaphylaxis.' *Med. J. Aust.*, vol. 1, 1977, p. 793.

81 Sutherland, S. K. 'Treatment of snake-bite in Australia. Some observations and recommendations.' *Med. J. Aust.*, vol. 1, 1975, pp. 30–32.

82 Fairley, N. H. *Prices Textbook of the Practice of Medicine.* 9th Edition, Oxford University Press, 1956, p. 342.

83 Sutherland, S. K. 'Antivenoms: Better late than never.' *Med. J. Aust.*, vol. 2, 10 December 1977, p. 813.

84 Hood, V. L. and Johnson, R. Commonwealth Serum Laboratories literature accompanying antivenom, 1978.

85 Sutherland, S. K. 'Snake bites and antivenoms.' *Australian Prescriber*, vol. 3, 1979, pp. 84–87.

86 Commonwealth Serum Laboratories. Literature accompanying antivenom.

87 Hood, V. L., and Johnson, J. R. 'Acute renal failure with myoglobinuria after Tiger snake-bite.' *Med. J. Aust.*, vol. 2, 1975, pp. 638–41.

88 Harris, A. R. C. *et al.* 'Renal failure after snake bite.' *Med. J. Aust.*, vol. 2, 1976, pp. 409–11.

89 Sutherland, S. K. 'Rapid venom identification: Availability of kits.' *Med. J. Aust.*, vol. 2, 1 December 1979, pp. 602–3.

90 Sutherland, S. K. 'Venomous Australian Creatures: The Action of Their Toxins and the Care of the Envenomated Patient.' *Anaesth. Intens. Care.*, vol. 4, 1974, p. 316.

91 Stackhouse, J. *Australia's Venomous Wildlife*. Paul Hamlyn Pty Limited, Sydney, 1970.

92 Morris, R. and Morris, D. *Men and Snakes*. McGraw Hill, New York, San Francisco, 1965.

93 Caras, R. *Venomous Animals of the World*. Prentice Hall, Englewood Cliffs, 1974.

94 Edwards, S. *New Idea*, 27 October 1979.

95 Venom research in Australia. Editorial, *Med. J. Aust.*, vol. 6, 5 April 1980, p. 293.

96 Sutherland, S. K. 'Acute untoward reactions to antivenoms.' *Med. J. Aust.*, vol. 2, 17 December 1977, pp. 841–42.

97 Sutherland, S. K. and Lovering, K. E. 'Antivenoms. Use and adverse reactions over a 12 month period in Australia and Papua New Guinea.' *Med. J. Aust.*, vol. 2, 1979, pp. 671–74.

98 Trinca, G. F. 'Treatment of snake bite.' *Med. J. Aust.*, vol. 1, 1963, pp. 275–80.

99 Sutherland, S. K. 'Serum reactions: An analysis of commercial antivenoms and the possible rate of anticomplementary activity in *de-novo* reactions to antivenoms and antitoxins.' *Med. J. Aust.*, vol. 1, 1977, pp. 613–15.

100 Campbell, C. H. 'Clinical aspects of snake bite in the Pacific area.' *Toxicon.*, vol. 7, June 1969, pp. 25–28.

101 The *Sun*, Monday, 14 May 1979, p. 3.

102 Storr, G. M. 'The genus *Notechis* (Serpentes: Elapidae) in Western Australia.' *Rec. West. Aust. Mus.*, 9(4), 1982, pp. 325–340.

103 Banks, C. 'Notes on seasonal colour change in a Western Brown Snake.' *Herpetofauna*, 13(1), pp. 29–30.

104 Mirtschin, P. J. 'Seasonal colour changes in the Inland Taipan *Oxyuranus microlepidotus* McCoy 1879.' *Herpetofauna*, in press.

105 Mirtschin, P. J. 'Double egg laying of *Oxyuranus scutellatus scutellatus*.' *Aust. J. Herp.*, in press.

106 Mirtschin, P. J. 'Occurrence and distribution of the

Inland Taipan *Oxyuranus microlepidotus* (Reptilia: Elapidae) in South Australia.' *Trans. Roy. Soc. of S.A.*, vol. 106, pt 4, pp. 213–214.

[107] Shine, R. 'Ecology of the Australian Death Adder *Acanthophis antarcticus* (Elapidae): Evidence for convergence with the Viperidae.' *Herpetologica*, 36(4), 1980, pp. 281–289.

[108] Gow, G. F. *Australia's Dangerous Snakes*. Angus & Robertson, Sydney, 1982.

[109] Storr, G. M. 'The genus *Acanthophis* (Serpentes: Elapidae) in Western Australia'. *Rec. West. Aust. Mus.*, 9(2), 1981, pp. 203–210.

[110] Smith, L. A. 'Variation in *Pseudechis australis* (Serpentes: Elapidae) in Western Australia and description of a new species of *Pseudechis*.' *Rec. West. Aust. Mus.*, 10(1), 1982, pp. 35–45.

[111] Information supplied by M.C.M. Biolabs Pty Ltd, Box 118, Blackburn, Victoria, Australia 3130.

INDEX